Learn to Love not to Hate
Now You Have A Place In The World Not Just In My Heart

Valerie Ann Hobbs

authorHOUSE

AuthorHouse™ UK Ltd.
500 Avebury Boulevard
Central Milton Keynes, MK9 2BE
www.authorhouse.co.uk
Phone: 08001974150

© *2009 Valerie Ann Hobbs. All rights reserved.*

No part of this book may be reproduced, stored in a retrieval system, or transmitted by any means without the written permission of the author.

First published by AuthorHouse 3/17/2009

ISBN: 978-1-4389-2884-5 (sc)

Printed in the United States of America
Bloomington, Indiana

This book is printed on acid-free paper.

Contents

Chapter 1. The Lump on the Knee..1

Chapter 2. My Sister and the Fire..3

Chapter 3. Dad Going Mad..8

Chapter 4. Mum Going Shopping...12

Chapter 5. Dad At His Worse..15

Chapter 6. Dad and the Puppies...20

Chapter 7. Nightmare at the Dentist..23

Chapter 8. Elwins Short Life...27

Chapter 9. My Dad and the Spade..29

Chapter 10. The children's home at East Dereham.......................32

Chapter 11. Survival of the Fittest..40

Chapter 12. Day Trip to Hunstanton..48

Chapter 13. The pains of Fishing..51

Chapter 14. The Punishment Room...54

Chapter 15. School days and school friends..................................57

Chapter 16. After Mum Remarried..68

Chapter 17. Good and bad times at the Bank...............................77

Chapter 18 (Part One). Summer at Aunt Nell's.............................82

Chapter 18 (Part 2)..89

Chapter 19. Caught at the swimming pool...................................96

Chapter 20. Wilburton school and myfriend Carol....................101

Chapter 21. Working at Mrs. Lamps...104

Chapter 22. The Start, Middle and End of
Mums and Dads Life 115

DEDICATION

I dedicate my book first of all, to my brother Elwin who was taken from me at a young age of 20 months old. People become silent of little Elwin, as if he never existed. Through those poor and dreadful times he gave good memories of which I have of my childhood. Elwins blond curly hair and big blue eyes will always stay with me, I love you to bits Elwin, and you'll always have a space in my heart. I would love to find his unmarked grave which is on waste land, so I could put a special gravestone on it, with two little cherubs, so they can look after him until we meet again one day and I can be the big sister he never had. The second thing I would like to dedicate my book to is all the children out there who are suffering torture and cruelty of evil abuse. In the hope of the book to be an inspiration, to the children suffering or have suffered, so that this book can give them hope and that they can find the strength, not to let the evil claim and ruin their futures. My saying " Learn To Love Not To Hate " is having a strong belief that God would always give me the strength to see the light at the end of the tunnel, It has got me through such hard times. Writing this book is like an end of a chapter; never will it be forgotten or taken from me, or the others he abused. But to put a closure that some may call Justice.

Dedicated to
Elwin Joseph Winters
-1953-1955

"Now you have a place in the world not just in My Heart"

Acknowledgement

First of all, I would like to give my warmest thanks to my beautiful daughter Gemma, for kick starting my life's ambition by writing the first few pages of my book for me. I would also like to say a big thank you for the hours spent typing up my stories and for driving me all those miles into rural Cambridgeshire and Norfolk in the name of research, and gathering all the photographs. I would also like to thank my loving Husband Roger, for the long hours spent converting the spare bedroom into my office for a Christmas present to encourage me to start my book, and I would also like to thank him for converting my thoughts into stories, and spending countless hours writing them down. Also I would like to extend my deepest thanks to my lovely son Thomas, for patiently reading my stories and the endless hours at the computer putting the stories onto disc to send to my publisher. I would also like to give my love and thanks to my oldest daughter Sherryie for reading the stories and giving her opinions and I would like to give my love to her Husband and my lovely Grandchildren, Kerri, Aaron and little Valerie. I would also like to extend my thanks to my sister Diane and her Husband Bill over in Southern Ireland for the love and good luck messages and for the blessing to go ahead and write my book.

Chapter 1
.The Lump on the Knee.

I shall start my life story with one of my earlier memories, I remember I was only a small child and I was sitting on a old wooden chair which drowned me in size as I was only a small unnourished child, I remember the house was very damp and cold, the house was very basic as we did not have much money.

I remember looking down and noticing something sticking from my knee, it was a sore red lump, my father noticed me looking and touching the red lump as I was very concerned about it, I was very curious to what this thing was bulging out my little frail leg. I never would have told my father, due to the fact I was very scared of him and his reactions if I told him. Father glared at me with his mysterious eyes. As he turned round he started approaching me suddenly and slowly across the cold floor boards.

When he approached me he glared down at me and I looked up into his piercing eyes, he picked me up like a rag doll, I was all skin and bones. Staying silent as I was unsure what was going to happen. Father marched into the kitchen with me under his arm, as I looked into his face there was no expression, just silence. He looked at me like he had just picked up a lifeless piece of wood; he had no compassion for me at all. As we entered the kitchen dad lumped me onto a rough and hard table which was placed in the middle of the room. Still unsure as what dad was going to do I froze like ice.

Next dad went and picked up a bread knife, I was hoping and praying dad was going to cut off a slice of bread and give it to me but that was unlike my dad. Dad proceeded and cut the lump off my knee, it was an unbelievable pain I cannot explain. As I fought the pain it got too much and slowly tears fell from my big brown eyes, one by one the tears escaped running down my little pale cheeks. I never screamed or made a noise as I would not let dad have the pleasure of hearing me in pain, I was far too strong minded even as a little child, but that was the one thing that got me through my saddening ordeals.

I never knew why dad was always so cruel to me but knowing no different I thought this was normal treatment. There was blood running off the knife onto my knee like heavy rain and dad just glared at me as if to say what he had just done was a good thing, and he expected me say thank you. Father then put the knife down, turned his back on me and slowly walked into the next room to return to mother and left me slowly to get over the pain.

Chapter 2
.My Sister and the Fire.

We managed to live in Silver street for two years, mother at the time was just waiting for another baby, not the best of times for dad to decide he is going to start making life more complicated by not paying granddad the money back which he borrowed to buy the house, we were now living in. There was a blunt argument about the money and dad refused in granddads face not to pay the money back, so granddad moved us out, well threw us out its more like, all thanks to dad's stubbornness that was the end of living in Silver Street.

But dad was never out of work long, he soon found another job, mind you having the gift of the gab probably had something to do with it. Everybody knew my dad as 'waggles', he was known as waggles as he was an Olympic liar. He also had a comment if people were right or wrong, it was simply a case of 'who you know and not what you know' everybody knew Ken Winters for their own good memories or more likely their own bad memories. Our next accommodation was in a little village called 'March', where dad had landed a job on the land; mum also got a small job on the land to help out as well.

The big manor house which we lived in stood on top of a big hill which overlooked most of March. I remember there were a couple of families as neighbors; the family who was much closer to us was called Mr. and Mrs. Galloway. I don't know if our presence there was known as a needy or even poor family but you could sense that's how it came across I imagine to others. Our neighbors 'The Galloway's' seemed very pleasant to our mum, I say our mum because they never seemed too fond of our dad perhaps they sensed what he was like. The Galloway's son was a very pleasant and bashful young man I used to like it when he came round to visit. He always used to bring round his mums freshly cooked homemade pies and bread but only when dad was out on the land working, perhaps he sensed we needed it more. Oh the fresh smell of freshly cooked bread which was still warm from the oven it was so appetizing, as you put the fresh bread in your mouth you could feel the hunger pain slip away as it melted in your mouth such a relieving feeling. I don't think the relationship between Mum and the son was only social but that was overlooked as the food was very welcome. We did not actually get much of the food as Mum wasn't very generous; we only got the slim pickings of the food donated by Mrs. Galloway, no chance we would ever get over weight. Mum used to save the majority of the food for dad when he came home and dad was never the wiser knew that mum did not bake it herself.

Not long after we moved in mum went into labor, Mrs. Galloway took mum to the maternity ward, were we waited for another unplanned child to join our family. Someone else to share our life of poverty and misfortunes . She soon gave birth to my new baby sister 'Diane Winters', I did not feel quite alone in this world any more. Mum soon came home and the first thing she done was place baby Diane on an old smelly green sofa like an unwanted parcel. The house we were living in was an old

Unloved farm house with big wooden beams coming down from the ceiling onto the floor, it also had big scary windows which looked over the fields, when baby Diane cried it used to echo around the whole house like a cave.

One morning I woke up and wandered down the stairs venturing down I could not even hear a mouse squeak , baby Diane was screaming and crying but that never bothered me , as when I heard her I knew I was not alone. I was stuck in this big scary house all by myself, there was no food and no heating; it was so cold it reminded me of the Antarctic. I had always been a survivor even as a child, so I constructed a plan. In the room was a big daunting Fire place. So I looked around and found some old scrunched up newspaper on the floor. So I picked

Learn to Love Not Hate

up the newspaper and started placing it on the Fire, when that was filled up I noticed there was some matches on the mantel piece above the Fire, so I reached for an old wooden chair and placed it against the wall to climb up and claim them. When I got down off the chair I lit a match and started the Fire. I have no idea how I had the knowledge to do this as I was only three years old I must have seen mum or dad do it in the past, you know what they say nothing like early learning.

That was one of the problems solved , Me and baby Diane were warm, I had my next task planned as baby Diane had messed her nappy, so I wandered into the kitchen to get a clean nappy for her, as she relied on me to look after her, after all we only had each other for survival. I eventually changed her nappy which was a hard task as I was only a small three year old child myself. Just when I had finished, baby Diane stared at me with her big green eyes, I knew at that very moment baby Diane felt relaxed as she had someone to look after her properly, in some ways I was like baby Diane's three year old mum, a task no three year old should have to have but I never had many choices in my life. It was never like baby Diane could rely on her mum or dad, as we were never wanted, we were just there.

I then sat on the mat next to the Fire with Diane; it was nice hearing her making noises which was not the sound of crying. An hour had past and there was a sudden bang on the door, it broke our peaceful silence, I promptly ran to the door to answer it, as I opened the door I was blinded by big shiny boots, I peered up and stared at a big stature of a policeman. The policeman glared down at me like a giant. He said softly "and what are you up to little madam, Valerie you know you should not be playing with fires". I smiled up at him as he was glaring down at me. I am sure the policeman knew we were at home by ourselves. As he looked around the house he foot tapped on the floor like a mighty horse walking around a stable. As he inspected our house he didn't say a word, he didn't even put the Fire out. Then I saw him turn and walk out the front door as he shut the door it made a slam. The policeman ventured down the lane to have a word with Mum and Dad, never mind the environment he had left me and baby Diane in. The policeman found my Dad and had a word with him about the condition me and baby Diane was in. The policeman explained to dad that he walked past the house and he saw smoke coming from the chimney and explained that I must have started the Fire as it was only me and baby Diane in the house.

Back in the house me and baby Diane were very hungry as we had had nothing to eat all day, I had managed to find Diane some old milk which was at the bottom of an old milk bottle, so that kept her content for a while. There was suddenly a bang at the door as Mum and Dad had come back from the land, there were steps coming from the kitchen which were over shadowed by dads voice "You should have locked them in their bloody Bedroom you silly cow, did you not think" Mum went straight into defense "it's not my fault they play up so much", I was so happy to see my parents return I was like a little dog waggling his tail, but dad just ignored me and Diane , They strolled upstairs to get away from us. Mum then walked across the old floor boards with an old wooden bucket of water to put out the Fire which I had made to keep us warm, mum was in a terrible mood as she turned around and stared at me like a animal would look at his prey in the wild, she marched towards me and picked me up, not for a cuddle which most mothers would do when they have not seen their baby girl all day. She drove me up towards the cold and depressing stairway as you hit the top, you could feel the temperature drop straight away, as it hit my soft pale skin. She then carried me , and left me in a small dark room and placed me on a cold bed, suddenly I felt a sharp painful hit on my back again and again, it was my dad viciously hitting me with his heavy metal belt off his trousers, as he was shouting" THIS WILL TEACH YOU TO PLAY UP,YOU THINK YOUR CLEVER I WILL SHOW YOU WHOS BOSS IN THIS HOUSE", all I can remember is screaming with my soft Childs voice as the pain was unbearable to deal with. Dad then dumped me on the bed and walked downstairs, when he reached the bottom he asked mum had she put the tea on.

As I lay on the dusty bed my strong will kicked in, and I lept up and rolled off the dusty bed, I then walked towards the stairway and gently sat on the top of the stairs, with my back still stinging from my Dad's savage attack. As I listened in carefully I could hear the two devils talking at the bottom, I had enough and went back for more. So I gently crept down the stairs, I could hear their voices get louder and louder, they were talking as if they just done the right thing to me. As I reached the bottom of the stairs, I stood there and mum saw me and came rushing over, as I was thinking "Oh No please don't hurt me again", she picked me up and sat me down and said "You Silly little girl I told you not to play on the stairs", it was as if she had a split personality and the women who led me upstairs to that painful assault was no longer here.

    She sat me at the table and we ate some food which looked like porridge, but I did not care as food was so hard to come across in our house. The stinging in my back seemed to fade away the more food I ate; it seemed to be the perfect remedy. At the end of the day, mum placed me and baby Diane on a cold bed upstairs as she left us, there was no emotion, no kiss no cuddle not even a good night, she just turned her back and shut the door. I remember laying there in so much pain but at least I was full up on the slop mum fed us, you probably wouldn't give that food to the pigs but I did not care, any food to us was better than nothing. As I lay there I stared into baby Diane's eyes and she stared back, I then reached for her little fragile hand and she held mine, I was so glad that dad hurt me and not her, as I knew I would always have comfort in my little sister Diane. We finally fell asleep holding hands it was so peaceful. My mum also had a little boy called Owen who was 11 months younger than me, luckily he did not have to go through these situations as my Nan and granddad took care of him, as mum could not manage three of us.

CHAPTER 3
.DAD GOING MAD.

In my early memories of being four years old, we were living in Witchford located near Ely. I was sitting on the cold and hard floor in the kitchen, I was watching mum all pale faced as she was proceeding with the washing , mind you the when she finished it, it looked no better but at least she was trying. Mum was using an old copper stick to do the washing, Dad soon walked through the door and mum straight away followed him like a magnet into the next room whilst carrying the copper stick.

The door then slammed shut behind them and I took it as a hint, so I just sat on the kitchen floor in my own little world. All of a sudden instant shouting came from the room "AHHHHHH, NO STOP!!!" Mums voice was echoing around the house, I have no idea why dad done these things to mum, it was just part of dads cruel and unexplained nature. He had pinned my mum down on the floor with his hand gripped so tight around her neck drawing the breath out bit by bit ,mum was trying her best to fight back but her struggles was not helping her situation. With his other hand Dad was shoving the copper stick up mums private again and again; the screams from mum were unbearable the sounds made me deeply sick. It continued for a little while then the sound of sorrow and pain stopped and dad vanished, the act he had committed was deeply sick.

I softly walked towards the door and poked my head round; the sight was deeply unpleasant; Mum was on her knees with tears falling heavily from her face. Each tear was like glass bottles of pain as they hit the floor you could hear a crash, all this to see was too much for my innocent child's eyes, and I had just heard and seen the work of the Devil. The atmosphere was truly terrible and I could feels mums pain in the depth of my stomach, I always felt like I was a adult in a Childs body and I'm sure if I had a adults body I would have ran in and threw the Devil off my Mum but I have always been handicapped by my size, my determination always outweighed my size. As I was standing there watching in deep silence, Mum go through this terrible ordeal there a deep man's voice coming from the front door, from the relief In the back of my head it was a policeman. The neighbors must have got concerned by all the bashing and shouting and called the police.

I wondered towards the front door and the policeman pushed me to one side and burst in, mum was crouched over holding her stomach in deep pain, the policeman stared in disbelief as the situation was getting worse, there was a thick stream of blood running down her legs, Mum was in a serious state. The policeman stood over Mum in complete disbelief, all of a sudden Dad returned and saw the policeman there, he saw him, turned around and in a wink he vanished, leaving mum in a terrible state and the policeman in complete disbelief. A few seconds later I heard police sirens racing down the street. The emergency team was helping Mum in the back of the ambulance, As I watched Mum get carried into the ambulance, I shouted with my arms stretched out in front of me "MUM, MUM", Mum just stared at me with eyes of blunt content, I loved my Mum so much but she never showed me any sign of concern or love back. The old fragile little lady came round from next door; as soon as she walked in I ran and hid under the dining table. I was so petrified, I was hiding because I was scared that I would get hurt. The fragile old lady bent over and said to me in a reassuring voice "come with me young lady let's get you away from this mess, you have seen too much already, good job you are only a child, you will not remember this painful view of torture" I wish that little old lady was right but unfortunately that painful sight has stuck with me to this very day. I think the old lady was underestimating the human mind, fifty years on I still have images of my father mistreating my Mum.

I grabbed the old lady like a baby chimp would its mother for protection, but I never knew how long that protection would last.

As me and the lady walked through my Mum and Dad's house it had suddenly turned from a war zone into a ghost town, As we walked through the house only the walls knew the truth of what really happened, it was as if the truth was plastered on the walls like wallpaper. As we walked through the room it reminded me of the tales of torment I had just gone through. As she opened the heavy wooden front door, there was beam of sun light hit are faces, the dull sky began to smile again. I looked over her shoulder as she was holding with a protective grip, I could see the big built policeman chasing after us, he was huffing and puffing, he finally caught us up shouting "MISS,MISS"," you'll have keep the child with you tonight, that bloody Ken Winters has ran down to the green where the big lop sided oak tree is." that old tree always reminded me of a face the bark was shaped with eyes and a mouth. Of course the tree could not talk it was a tree. I always had a runaway imagination as a child. My mind probably ran away so much as I knew no one could abuse my thoughts or ideas, I knew they would always be untainted no matter what happened to me. Even though I am in this horrible world where nobody wanted me, I could imagine myself away and dream of a better life. I never wanted a life of living in a castle with plenty of toys and being rich, all I wanted in life was to have some people's time and to be noticed.

The police chased my Dad down the lane and were trying to arrest him for the assault he had just done on Mum, Dad had climbed up the old oak tree and was shouting down, at the top of his voice " I WILL COMMIT SUICIDE" he was shouting at the top of his voice " I GOING TO DO IT,I WILL JUMP OFF THE TREE AND KILL MYSELF" the police got Dad down with a lot of struggle, they had had enough of playing Ken Winter games, he was then sent to Forborne in Cambridge. He was committed to a mental hospital. They used to send people with mental health problems there in those days. I stayed with our neighbor for a couple of days, I never minded as I was fed regularly and always kept warm. The feeling of a full belly felt so foreign to me but it was certainly welcome. I also got some acknowledgement; My own parents could not even give me that. It was not very clean in the house and there was a smell of dry heat, but I could easily put up with it, Compared to our house this was a palace. I had never seen so many

Learn to Love Not Hate

people before, for at least a couple of days I had felt what it was like to be a proper little girl.
I had no worry about being hurt or waiting for my father to come and take me from my bed, but I spoke to soon and tempted fate.

Mum came and collected me from the fragile and generous old lady, mum did not seem too pleased to have me back, but at least I had a break from hell for a couple of days. A week passed and no sign of my Dad appearing, nothing changed; Mum was in doors moping about the house. I was sitting on the living room floor, and then Granny walked past our house. She was a lovely lady, not very tall nor skinny, she was kind of short and dumpy but not fat. She had a lovely smile which could light up the sky. Mum stuck her head out of the window"He's coming out you know, I have got him out you know" she shouted to Nan, Nan did not say a word and continued to walk on, Nan was not a big fan of dad. Mum then slammed the window. I had no idea why Mum kept letting dad get away with it, was it fear or was it true love, I just did not know. The only person who knew the answers was Mum, perhaps she was scared to be alone or maybe she was the one who was ill in the head. I know I would never find out, I just had to live with the decisions she made

Chapter 4
.Mum Going Shopping.

I remember one particularly hard time in my life, it was 1954 and I had just turned four. I recall I was playing in the kitchen with my younger sister Diane and my baby brother Owen. The kitchen door was wide open and I could hear my dad snoozing away, he was having a sleep in his favorite arm chair, I could see through the door that mum was also in the room standing in front of the Fire place looking into the big wooden framed mirror, which hung on an old rusty chain above the mantel piece. I crept up to the doorway and watched mum brush her long black hair, putting each piece in place and placing a hairgrip over it.

You could see on her face that this part of the week was her favorite as she looked really happy. It was Thursday the day of the market in Ely and Mum was going shopping. I watched her as she applied her lipstick and putting her earrings in one by one. I have to admit she looked like a Film star when she made the effort. I could not make out in my young mind why she went to all this effort just to go shopping, and why she used to go out after dinner and that would be the last time I would see her for the rest of the day. On Thursdays she cared about us even less than any other day of the week, she classed us all as mistakes anyway.

On Thursdays she left our father to look after us, it was also the happiest we saw him all week, he didn't seem to care that she was going 'shopping '. Just before she was about to leave she would wake father

Learn to Love Not Hate

up and say goodbye and tell him to put us to bed when he was ready. He was ready as soon as mum walked out the door. He would put us in bed just to get us out the way; he didn't want us for companionship. He would quickly give us a slice of stale bread and a hard lump of cheese, with a glass of cold water. After we had finished this poor offering, he would march us upstairs, leaving Owen in his pram downstairs in front of the warm fire. As soon as we got upstairs he snarled at me and Diane "get to the bedroom and get into bed," he added in a nasty tone "if I hear any noise from you, it will be all the worse for you." mine and Diane's bedroom was not a very nice place, there was probably nicer sheds down on the old allotments, there was no curtains up on the windows and no carpet on the floor, just rough dusty floorboards. There was a massive bed in the middle of the room and a very large wardrobe in the corner.

There was not anything which you would find in a normal Childs bedroom, no toys no books and certainly no television, but we did find a novel way to entertain ourselves. At the end of the bed there was a brass bar with two brass balls attached. Diane and I used to unscrew the balls and use them as a form of a marbles. I remember me and Diane made up this little rhyme "Look at the bed get some bread ,look at the floor, get some more, look at the door, I want some more." me and Diane used to sing this as we rolled the balls across the floor trying to fill our stomachs up with the words of the song. We would play with the brass balls, As we started to get a little tired, we would then gently screw the balls back on the bed and pull back the dark shaded blankets from the bed, they were really heavy with dampness. We would then roll back the sheets which were grey instead of being white due to oldness; they also felt as stiff as cardboard. We would then climb into bed fully clothed, then figit away trying to get ourselves warm.

The bedroom was like a fridge and you could see the steam come from our mouths as we breathed in and out. We had been in bed for ages and we had just drifted off to sleep, when I was awoken by the sound of creaking floorboards and heavy footsteps coming up the landing. I saw the door knob moving and slowly the door opened, I thought to myself "oh, no here we go again", I saw the big shadow creeping across the bedroom floor by the light of the moon coming through the window. I then felt my sheets being pulled back and a pair of big rough hands picking me up followed by a deep voice saying" come on Valerie time to play are little game" he was trying to be nice. He then carried me gently down the dark and eerie landing, towards his bedroom. My poor little heart was pounding like a bass drum, as he laid me on his bed.

I was so scared; I was shaking like a little leaf and it then when I messed myself. I had tears running down my face. My father then removed my knickers and cleaned me up and it was at this point that my dad turned into the Devil, he must have got some thrill out of all of this. He then laid me in his bed after taking the rest of my clothes off. The Devil then got in beside me, I then felt his hand go up and down me it felt like a big piece of sandpaper, reaching places they shouldn't, I also felt his other arm go up and down as he laid there heavy breathing playing with himself. At that time being only a small child I had no idea of the perverse pleasures he was getting out of this. Being so small I was helpless in this situation. After awhile Dad had finished and whispered in my ear " don't tell mother about the game we have just played, it's our little secret" he told me if I ever told mum I would be taken away and locked up for being naughty.

He would then pick me up like a rag doll and carried to my bedroom, he pushed me through the door and shut it without saying goodnight or nothing, and he then walked off in silence. I crawled back into bed, shivering and shaking, watching the big scary tree branch hit against my bedroom window, it was like a big scary monsters arm. I lay there for ages not understanding the game we had just played, and wondering what I had done what was naughty. I had no idea what normal was at my age, Anyway I eventually nodded off in the end, only to awoken by my Mum, when she got back from shopping. There would be a lot of shouting and arguing, perhaps Mum had over spent I don't know. Sadly this used to be a regular Thursday thing for quite a while.

Chapter 5
.Dad At His Worse.

Back in the days when I was Five years old, my Mum and Kenneth my dad were living in a very old cottage near a farm on the outskirts of Chatteris in Cambridgeshire. They were both very young as my Mum was 23 and my Dad only being 24; they were struggling to bring up 3 kids born very close together. There was Me, my brother Owen and my baby sister Diane. Times were hard and both my mother and my father had to work, on the farm. My father worked very long hours and my mum fitted in part time work when she could. The cottage we were living in was very isolated, it was down the lane from the farm and there was only a couple of houses down the lane, in them houses lived a couple of young families, one of those families were called the Galloway's, I can't remember the other families names. The cottage we lived in was very old and run down with no electric and no toilets, we had to use the toilet outside in the shed or at night times we had to wee in a bucket.

I remember one day I was outside playing in a ditch with a couple of boys and I saw my father coming down the lane on his bicycle with his gun on his shoulder, I started waving and shouting as I was so happy to see him, as he rode past he took his hand of the handlebar and pointed towards the house. I got out of the ditch and started running back to our cottage. When I got back inside dad was standing there looking very cross, he then took off his belt and grabbed me, he then threw me across a chair and pulled my knickers down and started hitting me hard he was shouting "I WILL TEACH YOU NOT TO TELL THE OTHER KIDS I HAVE BEEN POACHING" I managed to struggle free and grab a heavy metal poker out of the fire place and then I hit him on the head, blood came pouring from his forehead, Mum came rushing into the kitchen and demanded to know what was going on, my dad who was absolutely furious slapped my mum round the face. My mum then grabbed me and rushed upstairs and tucked me into bed I believe she took me there to get me out the reach of father. I remember we were both crying our eyes out as we heard our father slam the door and rush out the house.

A few weeks later I remember coming home from playing with my friends, I went straight into the kitchen, my mum was sitting on a chair soaking her feet in a bowl of hot water, she had her skirt rolled up round her knees, my sister Diane was asleep in her pram and my brother Owen was playing on the cold lino floor, so I sat on a chair next to him and we started chatting for a while. After a while my Dad came home from work, he stormed through the backdoor in a really bad mood he must have had a really bad day at work, he did not say hello or anything. He took one glance at mum and shouted "WHAT THE BLOODY HELL ARE YOU DOING WOMEN" He then picked up the bowl of hot water and threw it all over her, mum was in sudden agony from the boiling water. Dad then stormed towards the cupboard and pulled out a carving knife and told her if she did not cover up he would shove it up her private. He then marched out of the room leaving a scene of utter chaos, there was water everywhere and everybody was in tears his final demands as he walked out was "MAKE SURE MY BLOODY DINNERS READY WHEN I GET BACK". Mum made sure we were all tucked in bed by the time he arrived back for his dinner. Later on that night I lay in bed listening to mums painful screams, as I believe dad was probably raping her again.

One day during one of my Dad's nastier assaults I heard my mum scream my name, she screamed out "Valerie go across to the Galloway's and get them to call the police, I think he is going to kill me". As I rushed towards the Galloway's, I did not make it as my dad rushed out the front door and cycled up the lane, the threat of the police must have really shook him up. Another time in November it was really cold and we were all around a roaring fire in the kitchen our Dad was with

Learn to Love Not Hate

us waiting on the arrival of our Mum as she had gone shopping in the local town, Mum was already an hour late back and Dads temper was getting worse and worse. After another hour Dad saw Mum struggling up the lane with bags and bags of shopping in her hands. Dad stormed out the house in a violent rage, he then grabbed her and dragged her screaming up the path with her shopping falling all over the place. Dad pulled mum into the kitchen and threw her into a big wooden chair, he then started shouting at her" about playing away and seeing her boyfriend" as this was going on he was holding the heavy poker over the roaring fire, my Mum was absolutely terrified and could not stop screaming "THE BUS WAS LATE, THE BUS WAS LATE" Dad refused to believe any of it and then he grabbed the poker out of the fire and started threatening her with it at close range. Mum was scared stiff she then made a plea for her escape and ran out the door, Dad then continued the chase with the flaming hot poker clenched in his hand. As this was going on a police car had arrived and three hefty police men got out the car and chased him, They trapped him in the back garden, where dad had cornered mum. The Galloway's must have sensed what was going on when all the shouting started. This time Dad could not escape the situation he had created, as the police sorted out the situation they told him if this ever happened again they would arrest him and takes things further, My Dad had escaped with only a police warning, but I am sure if they did arrest him there and then, they would have saved themselves a lot of trouble in the future.

I remember another time Mum and Dad were arguing over his shirts she had just cleaned for him, dad believed they were not clean enough and he started throwing soap bars and scrubbing brushes at her, whilst he was slapping her vigorously and shouting abuse at her. He threw one of the heavy brushes at her it clumped into her head and she fell to the floor, Dad did not hold back and he jumped on her fiercely and shoved the bar of soap in her mouth shouting "THIS IS A BAR OF SOAP YOU USE IT TO SCRUB MY COLLARS WITH". Poor mum was crying her eyes out, he then gave her a final slap and stormed out saying "if anyone one of you mention this to anyone, I will kill yar" you would have believed it if you had seen Dads tempers.

One day I was in the back garden playing innocently and mum called out "Valerie could you go into the village and get me a packet of fags" so I went inside put on my coat and Mum gave me the money and a note for the shopkeeper and off I went. It was about a two mile walk across the fields into the village, I eventually arrived at the shop, the shopkeeper was a friendly old lady, she had known me since I was only a small child in a pram. I gave her the note mum had written and she put the fags in a little brown bag, she also chucked in a few sweets for me and gave me a friendly wink, she told me to eat them before I got back home, I said my thanks and started my journey home. I had just finished my sweets and was nearly home near the lane and could hear my Mum shout "come on Valerie I need my fags" all of a sudden the local gypsy came roaring down the road in his lorry and knocked me flying. I was knocked unconscious; mum came running across the road to see if I was alright. She was screaming and shouting "VALERIE, VALERIE". Mrs Galloway must have seen the accident and called the ambulance straight away. The gypsy got out the lorry and checked me out, he covered me with his coat. After a while the ambulance arrived along with the local doctor. The doctor told my mum I had to go to hospital as I had cuts and bruises and suffering from a concussion. I was put into an ambuliance and taken to the R.A.F hospital in Ely, my mum came with me in the ambulance. When we arrived at the hospital,

They put me in the children's ward. After a long wait the doctor came along to examine me. The doctor remarked on how thin and undernourished I looked and said that I would have to stay in hospital for a couple of weeks to build my strength and put some weight on. The next day when mum came to visit me I noticed she had a cut on her forehead and a black eye, I found out later that dad did this to mum for sending me down the shop on my own. I remember one thing about the hospital and that was the baby in the bed next to me was swelling up twice its size like a balloon. That very night the baby died and all I could hear was the babies' last screams of agony.

A few weeks after I came out of hospital me, My sister and my brother all caught mumps, Mum wanted the day off work to look after us, but dad being his usual(caring)self told her "you must be joking we need the money" then he said "tuck them in bed until you get home at dinner", so mum being scared of Dad, Done what she was told, she put us in bed, locked the door and went off to work for us to survive by ourselves. After she was gone a little while Owen started crying, he was crying and said he was hot. I felt Owens forehead and he was burning up quick, I looked around for some water for him but mum had not left any food or drink. The only water I had found was in the pee bucket, so I had to give him some of that to drink then I wiped his forehead. Finally Mum and Dad arrived at dinnertime and then I told mum what had happened, on hearing this Dad exploded and slapped mum round the face and shouted "YOU SILLY COW YOU DID NOT LEAVE THEM ANY DRINK" I felt sorry for mum and wished I had not said nothing.

A few weeks later we all finally got over the mumps and then a couple of weeks after that I was back in hospital, this time I was suffering from tonsillitis and taken back to the R.A.F hospital in Ely where once again I needed building up again because I was weak and undernourished. Mum and Dad came and visited me every day and every time Mum had a new cut or bruise on her, When I was released and went home things seemed to get a little better and Dads tempers seemed to have calmed down. I learnt later that Mrs. Galloway had called the health workers and Mum and Dad were receiving counseling

Things seemed to be going better, but it all flared up again later on in our lives, as Dads evil ways were only floating beneath the surface and waiting for any excuse to errupt.

Chapter 6
.Dad and the Puppies.

I remember another time while we were living in that big scary timber framed manor house in the middle of the countryside near March, in Cambridgeshire. It was in the middle of winter and it was bitterly cold outside, Mum, Dad, Owen and I were all sitting round a big roaring fire in the kitchen trying to keep warm. My younger sister Diane was all tucked up in her pram sleeping soundly, the pram tucked under the stairs in the hallway, just outside the kitchen door. It was put there for her to keep her away from the drafts of which there was plenty. All of a sudden I heard my sister Diane started crying, she sounded as if there was something wrong with her. Dad said to Mum "Go Shut That Bloody Kid up will you." Mum got up quickly and went to see what she could do, she done this straight away because she did not want to upset Dad. Mum was out there a little while, but she could not do anything to settle her, so she came marching in the kitchen and snapped at me " Valerie go and rock the pram will you." So on I went into the cold hallway and started to rock the pram, it was that or a slap round the head.

After about half an hour little Diane, went off to sleep. Mum then let me back in the kitchen, so I sat back in the scruffy old sofa next to my brother Owen and tried to warm up again, after I had sat there awhile, I was desperately in need of a wee, probably because I had been standing in the hallway for a long time. I looked at Dad who was sitting in his favorite armchair smoking a cigarette, and then I looked at mum

Learn to Love Not Hate

who was enjoying a cup of tea. I thought to myself" I'd better not say anything because it will make them mad", that just proves how scared I was of the two, so I just crossed my legs and thought of England.

I sat there for about another half an hour and then I plucked up the courage and asked my Dad "can I go to the toilet please," Dad looked at Mum and Mum looked back at Dad. After a while Dad got up and grabbed me by the arm then led me roughly to the back door, he opened it and threw me outside and said" GO ON THEN YOU KNOW WHERE IT IS." he then slammed the door behind me, it was very dark outside and the toilet was at the end of a row of very old run down sheds. I looked around very scared, the wind was blowing and the branches were waving about, making the trees looking like big scary monsters. I crept up the path keeping close to the sheds, using the sheds to block out the aggressive wind. As I passed one of the old sheds I could have sworn I heard a dog bark, I didn't know we had a dog, I had never seen it anyway. I did not hear anymore barks, so I carried on towards the toilet, I eventually got there and I opened the old heavy door, then I sat down on the wooden seat. It was draughty in there and it smelled awful. There was no light in the creepy toilet either, I hurried up and finished my business, then started my journey back towards the house.

On my way back I heard the dog bark again, this time I knew I was not mistaken. The noise came from the shed I was standing right next to. Curiosity got the better of me, so I reached up and undid the latch on the shed door. As the door swung open the moonlight lit up the shed, there in front of me laying on a pair of old sacks was a lovely black dog, lying beside the dog was six beautiful puppies. I stood there in amazement and was just about to pick one up, when I heard Dad shouting from the back door "Come on Valerie What the bloody hell are you doing." when I heard the shouting I quickly got out the shed and shut the door, then made my way back to the house. When I got their Dad grabbed me by the arm and pulled me inside. I didn't tell Dad I had seen the puppies as I planned to go and see them in the morning. I sat back on the rough sofa with Owen, and then we were given a glass of milk and ordered to go and get ready for bed.

Owen and I then went upstairs to our cold bedroom and got inside our freezing beds with its damp sheets. I snuggled up and eventually got warm, then went to sleep that night dreaming of playing with the puppies. The next morning arrived and I was so excited, I woke and went downstairs, I went and sat down at the kitchen table as Mum and Owen were in the living room, they were feeding baby Diane. I was sitting there eating a slice of toast. I was sitting there staring out the back door as it was wide open, due to being a lovely sunny day.

Then I noticed Dad coming out the shed where I had seen the puppies last night. As he sneaked out the shed he had a quick look around, he was acting very suspiciously, he then came down the path, in one hand he was carrying a very large crowbar and in the other hand he was carrying a very large Hessian sack, to my amazement the sack was wriggling about, I sat there watching and wondering what on earth was he doing. I carried on watching him as he made hasty progress down the path. Dad carried on down the path until he came to a big metal manhole cover, I watched curiously as dad put the sack down and levered the manhole cover with his crowbar. I then watched in complete horror as Dad untied the sack and pulled out six puppies, One by one Dad without mercy dropped each one down the sewer. I'm sure I could hear each puppy make their last cry for help as they hit the water.

I sat there with tears in my eyes, as I watched Dad fold up the sack and replace the manhole cover; He then proceeded to walk up the path. I sat there scared and not daring to say anything, as Dad walked into the kitchen completely unmarked and with no emotion whatsoever. I carried on as if nothing ever happened, fearing I would end up down the sewer. What I saw that morning would scar my mind for ever.

Chapter 7
.Nightmare at the Dentist.

I remember going back to my early days and the time I started primary school, I recall being taken to school by my Mum. I was very nervous about going as I had never mixed with lots of children, my own age before. Mum had to half drag me there; when she got me there I was shaking in my boots, as I saw all the other kids screaming and shouting in the playground. Eventually we reached the headmasters office after fighting our way through the crowds in the playground. Mum introduced me and handed the headmaster my details. After a little while Mum said she had to go, so Mum left me in the headmaster's office and went through the door after giving me a peck on the cheek. I watched her with a lump in my throat trying to hold back the tears rushing out. The Headmaster then took my hand and led me to my classroom, where he introduced me to my teacher, who was a pretty young woman called Mrs. Butcher.

The Headmaster then left us to it. Mrs. Butcher then showed me to my desk where I would be sitting every day. Luck was with me as I would be sharing my desk with a shy ordinary little girl called Sarah, who turned out to be very friendly, she straight away said hello and asked my name, I told her, then she said she would show me the ropes as this was her second year at school. The day soon flew by and then it came up to dinner time, Sarah took me to the dining hall and a freshly cooked meal was put out in front of me. I stared at it with eyes the size of dinner plates; I had never seen food like it in my whole life. I enjoyed every mouthful of it, after all the fretting and worrying school wasn't going to be that bad at all. Anyway things went the same all week and me and my new friend Sarah got closer and closer. Then the dreaded weekend come, no school and no Sarah just mum and my awful father and the babies. Eventually Monday came and I met up with my friend Sarah at the school gates, As we went through the gates I noticed a big white caravan parked near the school kitchen," what's that big white van." I asked Sarah. She grinned and told me it was the dentist van, she told me it comes every six months to check all the children's teeth.

I had heard vague stories about dentists before when I had been listening to adults talking, the stories I heard made dentists sound like monsters and their rooms were like torture chambers. Anyway I started thinking of ways that I could get offschool for the rest of the week, as it turned out all that thinking was a waste of time, because at dinner time Mum turned up at the school, They were going to check all the new children's teeth first. All us new children had to form a line next to our mothers against the wall, and wait for our turn. After about half an hour a big fat women in a stained apron come through the door and said in a deep manly voice "Valerie Winters the dentist is ready to see you." I was shaking like a leaf as Mum dragged me towards the door nearly ripping my arm from its socket, Mum then shoved me through the door and said "Go on you little wimp, I will wait here." I nervously followed the fat women up the stairs into the little room, I was horrified by what I saw, there was leads and cables and two big gas cylinders, In the middle of the room there was a big black chair and above that there was a big light, standing next to the chair was a tall skinny man wearing big black thick glasses, and he was smiling at me like a Japanese solider. All the stories I had heard about torture chambers were true, the big fat women got hold of me and put me in the black chair.

I sat in the chair feeling like I was being eaten by a big black monster, I was shivering and quivering and pretty close to tears. The dentist told me to open my mouth so he could check my teeth, I opened my mouth and the dentist started prodding my mouth with his little hook, I Must have been shaking so much that the dentist must had stuck his hook into my gum, I yelled out in pain and lashed out with my foot. I must have hit him pretty hard as he yelled out as well. I saw the opportunity and jumped out the chair, barged out the van door, and then ran down

Learn to Love Not Hate

the van steps, Bright sunshine hit my face as I entered the playground, the big fat women was chasing me shouting "COME BACK, COME BACK," My mum then poked her head out of the backdoor trying to find out what all the fuss is all about.

When she found out, she grabbed me by the arm very roughly and dragged me through the school gates shouting loudly and slapping me around the head "You bloody little cow how you dare you embarrass me in this way." I fought and struggled all the way home and must have got a slap every ten yards, but that didn't worry me, I was just glad to be out that horrible white van. When we got home I was thrown into the house and sent to bed with no tea (again), with one final slap for good measures, as I was thrown into my bed. I was starving as I also missed my dinner that day due to the dentists, I was having terrible nightmares about dentists and black chairs, and I suddenly woke up. Soaking wet I had realized I had wet the bed, I lay there scared to death as it dawned on me, that if my evil father found out he would give a severe beating with his big leather belt, I lay there scared to death and thinking of a way I could hide it so he would not find out, finally the idea came to me that if I turn over the mattress then nobody would be more the wiser. So I got out of bed and dragged the blankets and sheets on the floor.

Then I wedged myself between the metal bed frame and the side of the heavy mattress, and after a few attempts and one last mammoth effort the mattress eventually flipped over and nearly fell in the right place. I then pulled the mattress a few inches to the right so it was in the right place. I then replaced the blankets and sheets and sat on the floor, with my knees tucked under my chin, sweating and completely shattered feeling very happy with myself and my efforts, after a while I had calmed down, I then climbed into bed, and fell into a deep sleep. Luckily no one ever found out as by the time mum had changed the sheets it had all drained through, good job she never changed them that often. A week after the whole dentist ordeal, Mum had gone out leaving Dad, to look after me.

I had another little accident as Dad could not be bothered to take me to the toilet, I had told Dad I had wet myself. He was not very pleased and called me a dirty cow amongst other things, he then told me I had better get myself upstairs and get a clean pair of knickers, so

I made my way upstairs feeling very scared, I approached my bedroom cupboard, where Mum kept my clean clothes. When I got there, to my horror Mum had put all my clothes on the top shelf, there was no way I could reach them, there was only one thing I could do, so I went to the stairs nervously and called down to my Dad to help me, Dad came storming up the stairs, I could see in his face he was irritated and angry, he said to me "Can't you do anything at all," he then threw me on the bed and ripped off my wet knickers, exposing my bare flesh. Then he took off that dreaded belt and proceeded to hit me, he hit me half a dozen times until he drew blood, he then picked up the knickers off the shelf and threw them at me. He left me there crying my eyes out; I was so bewildered by what I had actually done wrong. After a while I had calmed down and I put on the clean knickers, they soaked up the majority of the blood, then I crept downstairs and hid up in the outside toilets, and waited for Mum to come home. I must have fallen asleep as I was awoken by banging on the door; it was mum calling me in for tea. She probably guessed Dad had played up but she didn't say anything as she would have got a severe beating. I have always been scared of the dentist to this very day

CHAPTER 8
.ELWINS SHORT LIFE.

This is about the short tragic life of Elwins Winters, In 1953 before Elwin was even thought of, unknown to the him he already had two sisters and a brother, of which I was the oldest sister, there was also Owen and Diane. Unknown to us children our father was going into prison convicted of rape on a young girl. Our father was only 22 years old his wife June (Mum) was only 21 years old. June being left on her own to look after three children, all under the age of 4, she was very scared and confused, as this task was beyond her capabilities. It was then that I think she got a little too friendly with a young shepherd boy, who worked on the farm, where Mum and Dad lived. I think he must have helped Mum with the children, helped with food and done various jobs in and out the house. Unfortunately they got too friendly and Mum fell pregnant. When Dad was released from prison, he found out that Mum was expecting a baby.

Dad found out it was not his and he was fuming, so he gave Mum a sickening beating, this is where the sad story of Elwin begins. I am sure the severe beating brought the birth on early, and Mum was rushed into Bowthorpe maternity Hospital in Wisbeach. Me and my sister were sent to stay with our Aunt and Uncle and their little girl, they were both farm workers and they both found it difficult, looking after us and working long hours. My brother Owen was sent to stay with Granny and Granddad down on the bank. Me, Owen and Diane were sent back to our Mum after 3 months, Elwin was born on the

18th March 1954, at Bowthorpe maternity Hospital. He must have been an unhappy baby as he wasn't born normal; this must have been because Dad beat Mum up so severely when she was carrying him. My memories of Elwin are very faint, what I can remember is that he was a tiny little boy with blonde curly hair and he also had lovely sky blue eyes. His eyes were full of innocence and he was a happy little boy, and he always wore a big happy smile, I will always carry those thoughts in my heart forever.

My nightmare hit reality one Dark, gloomy and cold night. Me, Owen and Diane were asleep in bed, when we were woken up by painful crying. It was gut wrenching hearing them cries, Granny and Granddad calmly walked into our bedroom, Granny explained Elwin was crying because he was very sick. She told us to go back to sleep and not to worry; it was a strong indication to expect the worst. After a long and unsettling night we awoke to hear that Elwin had been rushed to Cambridge Hospital. 3 weeks later Elwin passed away leaving a few happy memories in my heart behind. The cause of death was Tuberculosis Meningitis, he finally left us on the 7th December 1955. He had left us but he will never be forgotten. He was only 20 months old, and it was a terrible time to go as it was coming up to Christmas, and this was meant to be a happy time of the year.

Back at home Mum and Dad had stripped the house of all clothes, all the furniture and all the bedding. They had to get rid of all of this because of Tuberculosis germs. Then we had to move to another house in Whitchford. Elwin was buried on the 21st December 1955, in Whitchford graveyard. The really sad thing is that he was buried in an unmarked grave, so it was like he never existed. My biggest dream and ambition is to find his grave, and then mark it with a gravestone with two little cherubs on it. This will officially give him a place in the graveyard and also proof he existed. So he will have a place in this world and not just in my heart. He passed away 53 years ago and I will always love my little brother.

R.I.P

Elwin Joseph Winters
1953-1955

CHAPTER 9
.MY DAD AND THE SPADE.

Another one of my earliest memories was from the time we were living in a very old cottage on a farm in Mildenhall, As Dad had decided to change his job again, and the cottage we were living in was very old and run down. The rain and draughts used to seep through the windows and the doorframe. The whole cottage seemed damp and cold and the paint was chipping off the walls, I remember it was summer time in the cottage, me Diane and Owen were very young and we had not started school, I recall we used to have a very large garden, which was surrounded with grass, when we were at Mildenhall , Mum and Dad used to have a pet dog, I can't remember what breed it was, but it was a very large dog with shiny black fur. She was a perfect family dog and great with us kids. Me and Owen used to play catch with her on them hot summer days it used to make the hours fly past.

Baby Diane was always asleep in her pram when we played catch, Our dog only had one fault and that she would always escape from our garden and venture into other peoples gardens, she was very adventurous, we would be sitting in our kitchen having our dinner and suddenly there would be a loud pounding at the door, and Dad would get up and answer it, when he opened the door there would be a sorry looking dog being held by the collar, on the other end of the collar would be a angry looking neighbor. He would tell Dad how the dog had ventured into his garden and started digging up his flowers, he would go on and on. Dad tried his best to hold his temper and then gave the neighbor a few pounds to shut him up. The neighbor would then march away mumbling something about "Bloody Dogs." any way this happened quite a few times and Mum started to give Dad a lot of grief about it, I didn't know how Dad did not lose his temper, but you could tell dad had trouble containing himself. Anyway after a few weeks after this ordeal, Dad finally lost his temper and during one of their many rows I remember him exploding with rage, and roared at mum "IM GOING TO KILL THAT BLOODY DOG", then he stormed out the room.

I don't think anyone took him seriously, because we all thought he loved that old dog, we should have known better as Dad did not love anything. One morning Mum told Dad she was going to do some shopping and could he look after me and Owen, Dad said he would. Mum then put her coat on and went off to do her shopping, after a little while of Mum being gone, Dad sat me and Owen on the kitchen table and told us to stay there and to be quiet. He then said in a soft tone of voice "I have to go into the yard and do a little job". He then gave us a cup of tea and a slice of jam on bread and slipped his coat on, then nipped out the backdoor, which he left slightly open. I watched out the crack of the door, Dad make his way down the yard into the old tool shed, After a while he made his way out of the shed holding a big rusty spade. He made his way up the garden towards the dogs kennel; I got a hard nervous lump in my throat.

As I watched him, I knew exactly what he was up to. Our dog was on the ground peacefully sleeping not bothering a soul, on the end of his chain. I watched in amazement and terror as Dad raised the big rusty spade above his head, and with one heavy thud, he hammered the spade down on her head without any care or remorse, Dad really was some kind of monster. There was one last sorry yelp from the dog as the spade roared into her head. Blood was pouring everywhere from her head, I watched with heavy tears running down my face, as Dad unchained her from the lead and dragged her like some garbage behind the old shed. He dug a hole very quickly and threw her dead body in it and covered it with dirt. I could not believe how quick this all happened it was a case of there was a dog and now there wasn't. Dad then came strolling back into the house humming away like nothing happened; I could not believe none of what I had seen. A couple of

Learn to Love Not Hate

hour's later mum returned from shopping and Dad greeted her and asked if the shopping went ok.

He then concocted a complete lie of a story, about how he went outside to feed the dog, and she must have broke off the chain and ran away. This man really was created by the Devil himself. We were all sitting there that night waiting for a knock at the door about the dog misbehaving, but me and Dad knew the dog was gone for good, I never could tell anyone about what I had seen that day because I always had a fear that I would end up next to our pet dog, 6ft down. I never told anyone about this, to this very day not even my brother Owen.

Chapter 10
.The children's home at East Dereham.

In the late winter of 1956, my father Kenneth was busy cultivating the land ready for sowing on his old fashioned crawler tractor in the bleak winter fields near March in Cambridgeshire. My Mother was stuck at home in the old manor house on the outskirts of a little village in the country side. She was alone with four young children, me aged six, my brother Owen aged five, my sister Diane aged three and my youngest brother Robert just one. It was starting to drive her up the wall only being young herself, Mother and Father had an argument, earlier that morning about something or other and he had gone to work in a terrible mood. Mother was very nervous for his return home, for the arguments would continue and she would end up getting a hiding, She was smoking like a chimney, she hit on the idea that she was going to leave before father came home. She made sure us children were safe and went round to the neighbors and old friends Mr. and Mrs. Galloway, to ask them if she could borrow the phone to call Granddad and Granny Winters who lived at the bank in Little Downham. When granddad and granny heard what mother was planning they dropped everything they were doing and got in granddads old black Austin car, They then drove to our house straight away. When they arrived at our house they found Mum very scared and upset and she told them she was planning to leave Dad. She wanted to leave straight away, she then

Learn to Love Not Hate

picked up little Robert and ran next door to the Galloway's. She had left me, Owen and Diane with Granddad and Granny as they stood in complete shock as what mother had just done. Mr. Galloway was seen putting Mum and Robert in his Water board Van, the firm he worked for.

It was learnt later that he drove them to Granddad and Granny Lyles in Broad street, Ely. Mean while granny Winters looked after me, Diane and Owen in the old manor house. While Granddad drove around in his car looking for our father who was working on the land somewhere, unaware what was going on. After a while father and Granddad arrived home. It was very dark when they got back so it must have been late, my father rushed out of the car and demanded to know what was going on. Granny Winters then washed us and settled us into bed for the night, We must have wondered what was going on. She then went downstairs to discuss with Granddad and father what they were going to do next. Granny and Granddad eventually got into their car and we heard them drive off back to the bank. When morning arrived Dad got us up he made sure we were dressed and gave us some breakfast. After breakfast my dad said" Valerie I think your hair needs a good wash ", I think this was just an excuse to get me alone, because as he put me in an old wicker wooden chair next to the stone sink in the kitchen, He said to me a low tone of voice" Don't tell anybody what I have done to you it's our little secret " I said in low Childs voice" No dad". later on that day there was loud knock on the big old wooden door, Dad answered the door and standing there was an official looking man and stood next to him was an official looking women, they said they were health inspectors from the local authorities. Father must have rang them up in the morning to arrange a Visit, they told my father they had found some places for us in a children's home in East Dereham. So in the space of 24 hours, we had not only lost our mother we were about to lose our father as well. Owen, Diane and me were then packed into the strange mans and women's car, dressed in the clothes we were wearing as we had no belongings.

Our father never said goodbye or gave us a cuddle, I don't know if he was even upset or glad to get rid of us. The man and women then got into the car, started the engine and drove up the drive. I looked back, I could not see my father, There was no waving, and no tears just an empty door step not even a shadow. We didn't know it at the time but that was the last time we would see the old manor house, the drive to East Dereham was very long and seemed like a thousand miles. We went on strange roads and saw lots of strange sights, it seemed like we were in the car for ever. When we eventually got to East Dereham, Norffolk. It was very late and very dark. The childrens home was not actually in East Dereham but was on the outskirts, in the middle of nowhere. We turned off the main road and drove through two big iron gates, and down a long gravel driveway. We drove for a while and parked in front a big creepy house, built of old red bricks; it looked like an old school house. This was to be our home for the next three years. The man and women then took us out the car and led us up big stone steps and through the front doors into a large reception area. We were then greeted by the house mother, who was not very tall and probably in her late 40s, she was also kind looking. We must have looked a very sorry selection of children, one blonde, one dark haired and one redhead. We were dressed in scruffy dirty cloths and we very thin and under nourished. She said come along my dears, let's take your names and particulars, after that we were took up stairs and had all are old clothes taken off us, by the house maids in separate bedrooms. We were then put in steaming hot baths, and scrubbed until we were clean.

    We were washed from head to toe, and our heads were washed with flea shampoo. We came out of the bathroom shining and smelling of carbolic soap. Dressed in clean knickers and a little dressing gown. We were then told to go into another room where we had to be seen by a doctor. I was first in and the doctor told me to remove my dressing gown, and get up on the couch. I was laying there in just my knickers, and the doctor started examining me. He noticed one of my ribs was sticking out more than the others. He asked me what had happened to it. I told him that my mother said it happened when my Dad was giving me a ride on his bike, when the handle of his beet hoe, went through the front wheel and we came off. I don't know if this was true or not, After the doctor had finished with us Diane and I were given clean skirts blouses and a little cardigan. Owen was given little shorts and a jumper. We were the taken downstairs to a fairly large dining room where we sat at a big wooden table and given a nice hot meal, with a steaming cup of tea. Our first proper food for nearly two

Learn to Love Not Hate

days. Little did we know at the time this was to be the happiest three years of our lives. Mr. and Mrs. Cave were the chief careers at the children's home. They were kind and caring people who looked after us really well, I do not remember much else about Mrs. Cave as she was probably doing paper work or helping in the kitchen, but I remember Mr. Cave talking to us a lot and he would come along and tuck us in at bed times, he was the person who taught me to say "Good night, God Bless And see you in the morning love you." After we had been at the home for a couple of months, and we had settled in. Our mother eventually found out where we were and decided to visit us; this was quiet an adventure as she had to change trains 3 times and had a long walk from East Dereham to the children's home. When she came on her first visit, after obtaining permission from Mr. Cave she turned up at the home, I didn't know wether to laugh or cry when I saw her.

When she saw us she ran up and gave us all a big cuddle, she told us to get our coats as she was going to take us to the pictures in East Dereham. When we got into town we had a look at what was being shown in the complex. It was a film about robots; we paid our money and went in to see the film. Every time one of the big metal men, with big red eyes came onto the screen Owen would run into the toilets screaming. When the film finished after a couple of hours, mum took us to the local café and brought us a cup of tea and a big cream cake, after tea we started our journey back to the home. When we got back we said are fair wells and after lot of kisses and cuddles our mother started her long journey home. After mums visits I used to get very ill, and upset and for this reason Mr. Cave didn't let Mum visit very often. While I was in the home I suffered badly from tonsillitis, they used to give me cups of Bovril and spoonfuls of Vile, which was a sticky syrup. They gave me these things to build up my strength, and put some weight on me.

I was fed those horrible liquids in the bathroom this was just in case I was sick or spitted it out, in the end they got me to drink it, I found it easier to swallow it rather than to have it forced into me, there must have been about twenty or so very sad children in the home, so there was loads of kids our own age, to get friendly with. If they did not want to know Owen, Diane and me always had each other. I remember the first summer we were at the children's home, we were told we were going on holiday to Great Yarmouth, to stay at another children's home for a whole week. When the date of our holiday arrived we were all packed into a mini bus and we set off laughing and singing. To go on holiday we were all given shirts which were yellow and blue checks. Along with those we were given grey shorts and a brand new pair of sandals, I had to have pair of boy's shorts as I was too rough with my girls pair, I kept breaking the zip in them. When then we arrived at Great Yarmouth on the Norfolk coast. After a journey of about an hour. We parked outside the home and were led in, we were shown our bedrooms we unpacked our few belongings we were then taken down stairs to the dining room were had a very nice supper. Then we were sent up to bed, as we were tired from the long journey, and all of the excitement of the day. For the rest of the week we done thing things that normal children with Mums and Dads would do, we played on the beach, built sand castles and went swimming. We were fed well at the home, we had a lovely dinner every night, and given a packed lunch to take with us during the day, the week sadly came to an end and we sadly returned to our home in East Dereham.

The week at Great Yarmouth was one of the happiest times of my life. During our times at the children's home we didn't go to a proper school instead we used to have a teacher who would come and visit us a few times in the week. My sister Diane was not old enough to go to school anyway; Owen was only just old enough. I remember some of the punishments at the home for being naughty, One of them was to be made to clean the other children's shoes, I was becoming an expert on cleaning shoes as I was naughty a lot of the time, another punishment was to send us to our bedrooms for the rest of the day, and not to be allowed to speak to anybody. They never used any form of corporal punishment on us or ever laid a finger on us. I remember every Saturday morning after breakfast we all had to line up in the dining room to receive are weekly pocket money of six pennies (about 2 and a half p in today's money). We all looked forward to our Saturday sixpence, which we could spend at the tuck shop, they had in the home. We would go and buy sweets chocolates or biscuits, this used to make us feel very grown up, being able to spend some money. Most of us in the home had never seen any money let alone spent it. Out the back of the home, we had a large field. On the field we had some swings and some climbing frames with a large sand pit. We spent a lot of time out on the field burning off excess energy, At the bottom of the field stood a old disused van, which had seen better days, we used to play in the van pretending it was a bus and we would take it in turns to drive it.

I used to think those were the happiest days of our lives. As we were fed well and there was people who actually cared about us, we never were cold or had to sleep in damp beds, we also had decent clean clothes and never had to wear dirty second hand ones, I can't remember are father ever coming to take us out anywhere, although he did come to visit us a couple of times, he came with Granny and Granddad in his old car, they came to see us but it was always supervised by one of the staff at the home. We were never happy about our father coming to see us, but we did like to see Granny and Granddad winters, as they brought little cakes and sweets as little treats. We used to like that a lot. We used to appreciate this as Granny and Granddad were getting old, I really loved my Granddad Winters he was lovely kind old man, but I didn't like Granny Winters as much, as she was very strict and very stern, the best time at the home were the couple of weeks leading up to Christmas, we would spend the days making paper chains blowing up balloons, and decorating the Christmas tree, which was put up by Mr. Cave and one of his friends.

On Christmas day we would wake up after virtually not sleeping all night, we would all troop down stairs into the dining room. We didn't have breakfast as we were all too excited. After a little while Mr. Cave and the rest of the staff, would enter the room, they were carrying sacks of presents. We would have to line up and we were given a parcel each, I would open my parcel with trembling and excited hands, as this was the first present I had received in my life. Inside my parcel was cute little black doll and a jigsaw puzzle. Diane opened her parcel she got a ball and skipping rope, then Owen got a little red tractor and a coloring book. After we had sat around playing with our presents Mr. and Mrs. Cave entered the room and announced it was dinner time.

We all sat down around two massive wooden tables, we sat eyes agog as a turkey the size of an ostrich was brought out. Mr. Cave carved the turkey and put it on our plates, with potatoes and vegetables, covered with lashing of steaming hot gravy. After we had eaten that, dishes of ice cream and jelly were brought out. We had never seen anything like this before, and we ate as much as we could. We all went to bed happy full up and with a lot of memories of the day, whilst I was cuddling my little black doll, my first ever happy little bed mate. After we had been at the home for three mostly happy years, three gorgeous summers and three marvelous Christmases, it was all about to come to an end. One morning Mr. Cave asked me to come and see him in his office, he sat me down on a chair and he told me that my Mum had asked him if she could take us home, she told Mr. Cave that she had set herself up in a house which her father had given her. It was fully furnished, she was working full time, but she said she would give up her job to be a full time mum. My father had also made enquiries into having us back to live with him, Mr. Cave asked me who I would prefer to live with, he was asking me as I was the oldest and the choice that I made would affect Owen and Diane, as they did not want to break us up. I didn't even think for a minute I told him straight away that I wanted us to live with our mum, and there was no way we were going to live with our father. After a few weeks of waiting we heard we were going home to our mum, before we were allowed home we were made to go for a medical examination, at this medical they found I had a weak left leg, they tried to use this to keep us in the home, but they decided as there was three of us they had better let us go home. After all the paper work was completed, which took a couple of days, Mum arrived to pick us up, after she had made the long journey by train.

We then packed are belongings and after a lot of tears and long goodbyes to all the staff, and Mr. and Mrs. Cave, we headed for the last time through the big gates and down the drive. Mum held our hands and walked down the station down East Dereham. When we arrived home in Ely, at the station it was starting to get dark and cold, as it was late October. We got off the train and headed passed rows of terraced houses, with the smoke pouring out the chimneys, when we got back home on the corner of Broad Street, Mum took us into the shop and told the shopkeeper who was also her friend, that she had just got us out of the children's home. The shop keeper bent down and gave us a big cuddle and gave us a bag of sweets each and wished us good luck, we left the shop and headed down Broad street to number 70, where Granny and Granddad Lyles were standing on the doorstep waving.

Learn to Love Not Hate

 They had been round the house early lit the fires and made sure the place was aired, after we had been back for a few weeks it was almost Christmas, and all the family were together again. The time flew past, my memories of our first Christmas back together was of our Mum creeping into our bedrooms in the middle of the night, and putting our presents on the end of our beds, she would then creep into Owens room and put Owens present on the end of his bed, we drifted back to sleep, only to woken a little while later by Owen shouting his head off, and shooting his guns, he got a cowboy outfit for Christmas, Diane and I got a cute little handbag each. I got a red one and Diane had a blue one, we also got a skipping rope and an orange and an apple this was our first Christmas at home.

Chapter 11
.Survival of the Fittest.

This is how we survived as young children in 1959. In Ely we had a river. A pub called the cutter and the quay, in those days we had a lot of holiday makers come down from Sheffield and from up north. They used to come down to fish for eels in the river of which Ely was famous for. They used to sell the eels for money, in the local pubs and guest houses, which they put on the menus. Me and my brother Owen used to escort the holiday makers across the river on a ferry, which was propelled by a chain. They used to pay us a sixpence a crossing, which we would go and buy sweets with at the sweetshop. The holiday makers used to rent the yachts and cruisers to go on the river for boating holidays. We used to be so hungry, that when the holiday makers threw their scraps in the bins on the river bank, we used to go to the bins and eat the scraps. When we were young we would go into town and pretended we needed to go to the toilet, we would then beg for a penny off the tourists. When we got the penny we would go round the back of the building and spend the penny on sweets instead. We all looked skinny and untidy; we looked liked old fashioned urchins. I remember we used to go around all the nearby fields and pick up all the old bones, which were left by dogs and people.

There used to be a big farm in the middle of Ely, and there used to be a lot of bones lying about. We used to collect all these bones and put them in a black sack, then take them down to the rag n bone man, who had a yard at the bottom of Broad street. He would then

Learn to Love Not Hate

weigh the bag, and then he would give us money for them. I remember one day Owen, Diane and me were playing in the park, when we saw this big metal manhole cover. We managed to pick it up and put it in the sack. The three of us dragged this sack down to the scrap yard somehow, I don't know how we done it, as we were all so small. We used to go round knocking on peoples doors; we used to pretend we were collecting clothes for jumble sales. When we got somewhere out of sight, we would sort the clothes out and keep the best ones for ourselves. The rest would go to the scrap man for some money. The scrap yard was large with dogs running about, it was run by a funny little man who had a horse and cart just like the programme 'Steptoe and son'. Next to the scrap yard, there was a row of derelict terrace houses, which were being renovated by builders. One evening when the builders were not working, my brother and I broke in and stole all the new lead piping, which the scrap man bought off us.

He asked no questions, we had another game where we would go to the local rubbish tip and look for things to sell. Sometimes we would be lucky and find boxes of cereal thrown out by local shops and supermarkets. We would all play in the rubbish tip, not knowing how dangerous this is to do, as there could have been hidden holes or sharp bits of metal sticking out, you could hurt yourself badly with. Mum never knew half the things we used to get up to, as she didn't really care as long as we were out the way. Another way we used to make money would be to go round and collect empty glass bottles, such as soft drink bottles. They used to charge a 3p deposit in those days. You would give them a 3p deposit in those days, then take it back at the end of the night and they gave it back. At nights we used to go round the back of the local pub, where they kept the bottles in crates, in a wire mesh cage, we were so skinny we used to reach though the mesh and grab the bottles. We would then take the bottles to the off license and collect our money, and then buy crisps and lemonade.

The off license manager never suspected a thing, he must have thought are parents drank a lot. We would also go round to all the local farms, and pinch all the free range eggs. The chickens laid them all over the place. One time we were looking for eggs and we went into a prefabricated building and we found a dead fox, lying in a dark corner. In those days there was a lot of wildlife lying about. The farmer must have thought it was the foxes nicking the eggs as we never got caught. On the allotments near Ely railway station there was an old shed we used to play in, one day we went to the shed with some eggs and some matches, we nicked from mum probably. We lit a fire and Owen tried to fry the eggs in an old sardine can. Someone must have seen the smoke coming from the shed and shouted out " OI ARE YOU TRYING TO BURN THE WHOLE BLOODY PLACE DOWN???!!!", He then chased us out the allotment, that was our little adventure for the day, Mum never found out about that either. When Owen and I were very small we had a friend called Graham. He and Owen went round picking up discarded cigarettes ends, from outside the pictures, and anywhere else that cigarette ends would gather up. They put the cigarette ends in an old tobacco tin they had, they went up the park and broke all the tobacco out of them.

They would then make a full size cigarette with some cigarette papers they had nicked from Grahams parents. The funny thing is this made up cigarette made Owen as sick as a dog, he has never smoked since. Ironical really as we spent our days looking for food. Mum was so cruel she kept us locked in the bedroom on Sundays, so she could lay in half the day. The only way we were allowed out was if we wanted to go to Sunday school. So Owen, Diane and I were especially keen to go, especially if was a hot summers day. When we were up and dressed we used to go down the road, right past the Sunday school and go straight down to the river. Using Sunday school as a excuse to get out the house. First thing we would do when we got down the river, was check the bins for breakfast (sometimes we were lucky), we would then walk down the river bank to check that the holiday makers had locked their boats up. If they were unlocked we would go in and check to see if they had left anything behind. On one occasion we were walking down the river bank and we saw a this large workmen's barge moored on the bank, Owen, Diane and I jumped aboard and entered the cabin which was unlocked, the workmen had left their tea making equipment on it, so we lit the stove and made ourselves a cup of tea. We looked out the window and realized the barge was moving, we all managed to jump off the barge onto the bank just in time. We then ran off home pretending we had been at Sunday school; I never did find out what happened to that barge.

Learn to Love Not Hate

When we did manage to get a meal at home we would sit around the table in the kitchen, and Mum and Dad would sit in the living room. They never wanted to sit with us. We always had cheap butter on stale bread; Mum and Dad would always have fresh butter on fresh bread. I remember when Mum and Dad would treat themselves to fish and chips they would shut us out the house and tell us to go and play, after a while Mum would come to the door and chuck out the fish skin and left over chips, when she shut the door, the three of would come along and eat the scraps off the floor, as we were hungry as usual. My Nan and Granddad Lyles used to live at No 71 Broad Street, Ely at the time, with our other brother Robert. Nana Lyles would sometimes give me a nice meal, not very often though. Me, Diane and Owen would go around theirs and watch their television, as Mum and Dad did not own one, nor did a lot of people back in those days.

I remember watching Bootsie and Snudge, Dixon of Dock Green and the News; these were Nanas and Granddads favorite programmes. Sometimes when I went round there Nana would wash my hair and plait it with bits of rag. The next day I would go round there and she would take the rags out, I would look like a Golliwog off the jam jars, as I had really black hair. This was one of my favourite times visiting Nan to watch the television, I loved my Granddad Lyles he was a lovely man but very strict. If Nanny Lyles would throw any scraps on the fire Granddad would moan at her and say she was feeding the devil. So she used to throw all the scraps over the wall for the birds. So along came Big bird Owen, Big bird Diane and Big bird Valerie and ate all the scraps on the way home. We did these things to survive not for fun.

A car similar to Grandads old black car

An old barge on the river in Ely similar tO the one's we played oN

Ely Cathedral

Wilburton School picture. Me fourth from Brother Owen second from right middle row.

Me and my sister Diane

The Grange Hospital in Ely where I was born

Ely River where we took the fisherman across on the ferry. The pub called the quay in the background.

Me on the beach at Hunstanton building sandcastles fifty years later

From left to right. Aunt Nells companion, Aunt Nell, Granny Lyles, Grandad Lyles

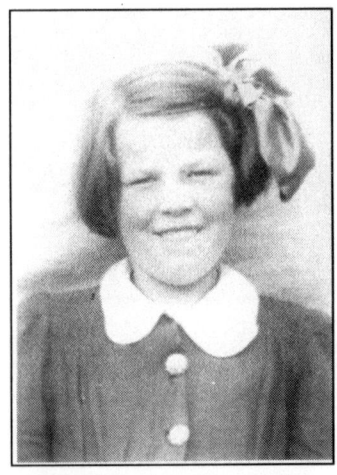

My Mum June Rose May aged 9

My Mums grave in Ely cemetery My Mum with my stepdad Herbert and my brother young Herbie

My old house 70 Broad street Ely where wE went to when we came out of the homE

The park we used to play in behind Ely Cathedral

This is the picture we had took to send to Dad in prison

My stepdad Herbert's grave in Ely cemetery

My sister Diane and me witH our mum down the seaside iN the 50'S

Chapter 12
.Day Trip to Hunstanton.

In 1959 when I was 9, me, my sister Diane and my brother Owen came out the childrens home where we spent three happy years, where Mr. and Mrs. Cave were the patrons. All 3 of us went to stay with our Granddad Lyles, who lived at number 70 for a while until they decided to buy the house next door. They decided to let our mum move in with the 3 of us in number 70 so we could live like a proper family. We moved in with our mother in to number 70, and this is when all the bad events started to happen again. Our youngest brother Robert who had lived with our Granddad and Grandma Lyles, since he was one years old, he started living with them when our Mum and Dad separated. Robert was now four years old and our Dad (Kenneth) got a court order allowing him to see us for an hour on a Saturday. On one occasion I remember Mum calling Granny and Granddad Lyles, to come and collect us as she was worried Dad was going to come round and give her a good hiding for something she had said or done.

"Well now we will move on to one of my better memories". One Saturday my father turned up with our Granddad Winters in his little black Ford Prefect. They said "we are going to take you all to the seaside." My mother said that would be alright as she was probably happy to get rid of us. We then went to our Grandma Lyles and picked up our little brother Robert, we were all packed like sardines in the little black Ford. It was a gorgeous summer's day, as we headed to our nearest seaside town which was Hunstanton, which was on the north coast. When we eventually arrived we ran straight down onto the beach.

While our Dad and Granddad (who was a loving little man) strolled to the beach shop and brought us a bucket and spade, and also some of those little flags. We made lots of sand castles and put our little flags on top of them. After we got fed up of making sand castles we went and had a swim in the sea. When we had enough of the sea, we collected our buckets and visited the rock pools, in the rock pools we collected our buckets full of crabs, sea weed and other such things that were found in the rock pools. When we had filled our buckets up dad brought us some fish and chips for dinner. This was the first time we had ever tasted real fish and chips and they tasted fantastic.

After we had finished our dinner, we walked up to the pier, which had lots of stalls and rides located on it. We had a couple of rides on a little carousel, which had horses on it; the horses went up and down, round and round. We were sitting on the horses eating our candy floss, and chewing our toffee apples. Our father Kenneth was a really good darts player, so he went and had a go on the darts Stall. He thought he would try and win me and my sister a doll each. I remember Dad taking out a really big five pound note, to pay. After a while and nearly all of his five pounds gone he finally won me and my sister a doll each. I had never had a real big doll before, so I was over the moon. The doll was made of porcelain and they were wearing really pretty dresses. They were also wearing little socks and shoes.

They had big eye lashes and their hair was painted on. After we had finished on the pier, Dad took us to a little café, where Dad and Granddad brought us some cakes and a cup of tea each. Which me, Diane, Owen and Robert really enjoyed. We were all really full up. Dad and Granddad then stuffed us in the car for the long journey home. Robert the youngest was starting to get really tired as it was a long journey home, and it had started to get really late. It took a long time to get home, in the little Ford as the roads were really bad in those days, as it seemed like we were travailing 100 miles to get home. Eventually we arrived home and Robert and Diane were fast asleep, Owen and me were over the moon with the day's events. Dad took Robert back

Valerie Ann Hobbs

round Granny and Granddads Lyles House, and he was put straight to bed full of happy memories. They then took the rest of us back to our mums, we ran up the path clutching our new dolls straight to our mum who was happy to see us (laugh), this was one of the happy memories from my troubled childhood.

CHAPTER 13
.THE PAINS OF FISHING.

I remember the summer of 1961. When I was just a little girl of eleven. My brother Owen and his friend Gordy and me used to go down the cutter on the river in Ely, Near the cutter Pub used to be an old Red brick wall, on which we used sit on and fish. My brother Owen had a real fishing rod with a proper reel but poor little me only had a piece of bamboo cane with a piece of fi shing line attached on and tied to the end I had the luxury of having a real fishing hook, Owen used to put the maggots on the end for me as I couldn't stand the wiggly little things, the sight of them made me feel sick straight away. On one occasion we were casting our lines into the river when our lines tangled and Owen being stronger pulled my bamboo cane straight into the river, I started shouting and crying as I was really upset, I suddenly stomped off home with Owen trailing behind me, I stomped into the house to find mum and explain the situation, at that time mum was going out with a man from Ireland, he was a typical Irish man with dark curly hair with Green eyes, his name was Mick or Brendon I can't quiet remember as I was just a child. He could see I was very upset so he slipped on his coat and popped down the shops, to my utter surprise he had gone and bought me a brand new fishing rod, I was so ecstatic and gave him a big hug.

The next day me and Owen went down to the cutter and settled down on our usual place on the red brick wall, to do a spot of fishing. Owen set up my brand new rod and showed the basics on how to use it, and then we settled down to fish. When we had been fishing for a while, I finally caught a fish and it was a nice looking fish as well, I started reeling it in, and with one mighty pull the fish came flying out the water and onto the bank, the fish started wriggling on the floor. Owen had to take control as the fish made me feel as nauseous as the maggots did; Owen had to take the fish off the hook. Then he reached for another maggot and put it on the end of my hook, as I swung my rod back to cast again the hook went around, then went straight into my knee, it went straight in past the barb on the hook, it was then I wished I had used a bent pin instead of a proper hook as I could not pull the hook out. So I went home with Owen as he was helping me, I was limping like a wounded soldier. When we eventually arrived home my mum saw the hook and said "Oh my god what have you done now." She sat me down on a stool in the kitchen and said "Don't move," she tried pulling and pushing the hook out, causing me to scream immensely, after a while she gave up" This is doing no good; I'm going to call the doctor." After a while the doctor arrived, he had a good look at it. He decided the only thing to do was to cut the hook off the line, and push the hook all the way through the skin, this really hurt as they did not numb it back in those days, this really put me off fishing.

I didn't go again for a long while. After a few months Mums boyfriend had to return back to Ireland as work at the sugar beet factory had finished for the season. He did ask mum to go back to Ireland but some reason I didn't know about she didn't want to go. As a result of this Mum became depressed and very run down, as she was a lone again looking after three kids and the house. I recall that Mum got some bad news concerning her friend Mrs. Galloway's son. He was the boy who helped us with food and random odd jobs around the house, when my Mum and Dad moved to March years ago. Mrs. Galloway's son was working for the water board in Cambridge, just outside of Ely. He was working in a water tower when he slipped and drowned, it was a big shock to everyone as he was only 29 years old, and this really upset my mother and made her really ill. Some close friends and neighbors noticed this and the Everett's called mum up and offered to let Diana stop with them for a bit as mum was too ill to look after her.

Learn to Love Not Hate

The Everett's had two children of their own; they had a son called Sydney who the splitting image of Elvis Presley, all the local girls really fancied him. They also had a daughter called Linda, who was not quiet all there. She was going to Wilburton special school which as a boarder of the school she was attending. This meant Linda's bedroom was empty and Diana could sleep in it, Diane only stayed at Mrs. Everett's for a couple of days, as she played up, rebelled and ripped all the wallpaper of the walls. Mrs. Everett marched Diane back to the house and told mum she was too much to handle. Later on Mrs. Everett had her own sad story, Mrs. Everett and her son Sydney decided to immigrate to Australia, Her husband refused to go, and stayed in England with their daughter Linda, Linda was 15 years old; even though she was backwards she did all the cooking and cleaning, while her father went to work. One night Mr. Everett died in his sleep, Linda must had thought he was a sleep and carried on with everyday chores, eventually after two weeks, his workmates missed him and sent an investigator round and that was the last I heard of the Everett's, Mum gradually got better and our lives continued.

Chapter 14
.The Punishment Room.

Towards the end of 1959 Diane and I caught chicken pox, which was going about Ely at the time, the pair of us were covered all over in irritating little spots, and confined to our bedroom. We were stuck in a little dark room, it was lit by mantel lights as there was no electricity in those days. Everywhere felt damp and it wasn't very cosy. The walls were covered with stained white wash and the room was painted in dark colures. The floor was covered in cold lino and there were no rugs or mats, and the wind whistled though the draughty old wooden windows past the threadbare curtains. In the middle of the bedroom stood a big brass bed with brass balls on each bed post. Up at one end of the bedroom stood an old fashioned dressing table with a glass flower vase standing on top of it, and in one corner stood an old wicker chair. Underneath the bed lay a big old suitcase.

When we got bored which was quite often we would unscrew the brass balls from the top of each bedpost and play marbles with them, we would sometimes lose them and that would earn us a smack around the ear hole, because that would mean mum would have to find them. We had been confined to the bedroom for nearly a week, with no regular food and only one meal a day, which our stepfather Herbert would bring up for us. We were stuck in the room with only our dolls which our real father won for us that summer, they were the only toys we had, not even any books. Outside the bedroom door Mum had put a bucket there so we could go to the toilet, Mum had warned us only to

Learn to Love Not Hate

use the bucket to go for a wee and not to do any big jobs, I don't know where we were meant to go for big jobs as Mum had locked the door at the bottom of the stairs. Sometimes when Mum had gone out our step father would sneak sweets in for us. One day Diane got really irritated after we had an argument, she got hold of my doll and smashed it, then threw it in the wee bucket, this upset me so much. Meanwhile Mum heard us make a lot of noise from downstairs, so she unlocked the door and came rushing up the stairs full of anger as usual.

On the way she had took a wooden stair rod off the stairs which was used to hold the carpet in place, she came rushing in the bedroom and only hit me with it as I was the oldest, Diane was only six. After mum left the room and went back downstairs I shouted at Diane and called her a little cow, and said it wasn't fair that she got me into trouble again, after that I went to sleep angry and upset. In the middle of the night I woke up and wanted to go to the toilet, unfortunately I wanted to do a big job, but I couldn't think where to go as mum had locked the door at the bottom of the stairs, I kept thinking what I could do and then in desperation I thought about the case under the bed, so I dragged this out quietly and squatted over it and done my business. I quietly shut the lid on the case and pushed it back under the bed. When morning arrived and mum came upstairs to check if were still alive, she said to us "What's that Bloody Awful Smell." We said we didn't know, so we started looking around and eventually pulled out the case from under the bed and opened it. She was so angry at what she saw and guessed it was me, she didn't even think of blaming Diane.

She shouted at me "YOU DIRTY LITTLE COW" and she laid into me beating my face and body, she then strode out the bedroom muttering and very angry dragging the case behind her, she slammed the door handle and we did not see her for the rest of the day. We heard the backdoor slam so we looked out the window we could see Mum drag the case behind her walking down the garden, were she left it and then came marching back into the house. It wasn't unusual being locked in the bedroom when we had chicken pox, because when we weren't even ill we would be locked in the room every night by 7'o'clock, we were expected to go straight to sleep and make no noise. This was virtually impossible as there were three pubs and a fish and chip down in our street, so it was quiet noisy outside and Owen was down stairs making noises as he was a nearly a year younger than me, he never got sent to bed early only us girls. If we did make any noises mum would rush up stairs and drag me out the bedroom and then shove me in the punishment room, the punishment room was a dark and cold room in the back of our house.

It had no curtains, no carpet and no blankets, there was a couple of metal boxes. She would lock me in there until she decided to let me go back to my bedroom; sometimes it might be a couple of days. One night when I was asleep, I woke up and desperately wanted a wee, I went onto the landing looking for the bucket but mum hadn't left it there so I went looking for the glass vase, but for some reason it wasn't there either. So I crept off to have a wee in the punishment room which was just along the landing, I had a quick listen and I couldn't hear anybody in the house. Mum and Herbert must have gone down the pub, so I entered the punishment room squatted down and had my wee. Too my horror I noticed my little brother Owen asleep on the mattress, he must have been sent there for something he had done wrong. Luckily he did not wake up. In the morning me and Diane were awoken by our mother shouting at Owen "YOU DIRTY LITTLE SOD, you shouldn't be wetting the bed at your age." little did he the know the truth, It's a good thing mum never knew the truth or else I would be dead. I wouldn't have wee'd on him on purpose it's just these little things we had to do to survive.

CHAPTER 15
.SCHOOL DAYS AND SCHOOL FRIENDS.

After we had our first Christmas at No 70 Broad street, after coming out of the children's home in 1959, it was early in 1960. Mum had to start looking for a school to send us to so we could start getting some education. I was nearly 9 years old, my brother Owen was 8 and little Diane was just 6. Mum found Diane a place in saint Ethereal that was a new girl's school that had not been built very long. Owen went to a boy's school not too far from our house, and I got a place in a girl's school, located in the middle of Ely. They had separate schools for girls and boys in those days. This was when my behavior problems were about to begin. I don't know why I was naughty, probably I was rebelling against the world, probably because all the things that had happened to me. I remember one day, I was playing around in the school toilets and I decided to fill all the sinks with water, so I put the plug in each sink and turned both taps on all until the sinks were overflowing and water went all over my shoes and socks. At that moment one of the old teachers was walking past and must have heard the water splashing on the floor.

The old women teacher marched into the toilets and shouted "Valerie what on earth are you doing, "she then dragged me out the toilets and into the classroom and took off my shoes and socks, and hung them on a rail next to an old pot boiler, which was run by a fuel called coke, which was smokeless form of coal. They used the pot boiler to heat the classroom in those days before central heating. The teacher then made me stand in the corner of the classroom, with my back to everyone. I then had a cone shaped hat put on my head with the letter

(D) Dunce written on it. Even when my brother, my sister and I were ill our mother made us go to school. On one particular day I felt really poorly and I was sitting at my desk shaking and shivering and the teacher asked me what was the matter, I told her what was wrong and how uncaring my mother was. Instead of sending me home, the teacher sat me next to the pot boiler, and she let me sleep it off. The teacher knew it would be a waste of time sending me home, I guess she must have cared a lot about me. I remember one day, I was at a loose end and I was messing about in the cloakroom. In the cloakroom there used to be some big wooden tea chests where they used to store books and things. That was not being used. I was bored so I started emptying the tea chest and then I started climbing in one to hide up. I got caught by one teacher and I got punished for that as well.

One day I remember a teacher told me that my mother was coming to pick me up; I feared the worst and thought she was going to take me back to the children's home. So I went around saying goodbye to everybody as I thought I would never see them again, what the teacher meant was that mother was coming to pick me up and take me home just like all the other mothers done as normal. My mother had never done this before, On Thursdays in Ely it was market day, and after school I would meet up with Diane and Owen and we would go and find Granddads black car, which was always nearly parked in the same place. I always remember the number plate which was DJE 591. Granny and Granddad would rarely miss the market as granddad always loved to do the Auctions, and Granny would love to look at the cows, sheep and pigs. They would always have their fish and chip supper on a Thursday. We would wait patiently by their car, when they eventually came they would give us a big hug, a bag of sweets and a little bit of money.

I stayed at the all girls' school in the middle of Ely until the school holidays began in July, and then I left that school forever. During the school holidays we would get up to a lot of things, such as going to the river. We would fish for tiddlers with a jam jar, attached to a long piece of string. We also had an old two wheeled metal scooter, which we used to go up and down the street, causing a lot of moaning and distress amongst the shoppers and pedestrians. Some days we would go down to the old sheds down by the railway station, the sheds used to have old concrete floors. We would whiz around on our big heavy metal roller skates, with big rubber wheels. We would go around and around until we had tired ourselves out.

Also during the school holidays the Sunday school would organize weekend trips to the seaside. In those days they would have lemonade and food for us kids, and for the grownups they would have crates of beer laid out in the gangway of the bus. Although our Mum never came on any of the trips. On the day of the outing we would be dressed in our Sunday best dresses and shoes and I would wear a little cotton dust coat. As we were about to board the bus, Granny and Granddad Lyles would come to wave us off and would hand Owen, Diane and me a shiny half crown. (About 12 and a half P) Granddad Lyles done this so mum could not take it off us. One of the places the Sunday school would take us was a place a few miles up the road from Hunstanton. There wasn't much there only a little shop, a few houses and a pub, which was handy for the parents. We would spend all day on the beach searching the rock pools for crabs, digging holes in the sand and paddling in the sea. The Sunday school would provide us with a packed lunch for dinner and towards the end of the day they would buy us an ice cream, and a cup of tea. Then we would all get on the bus, and head home singing songs.

We were all in a happy mood. There used to be a women who ran the post office in Broad Street, she used to have a big black Labrador, there was an old man called Ben Taylor who was about seventy. He would go around to the post office and walk the Labrador for her, as she never got time. When we saw him walking the dog we would go up to him and say "Hello," and then we would tell him it's our birthday, he would then give us a little bit of money as a birthday present. Every time he would give us some money he would say "Bloody Hell you have more birthdays than the Queen ", he was only joking he loved us kids really. Ben Taylor lived in a big house down by the river; he lived with his mum who was well over Ninety years old. After the school holidays were over and forgot about, it was time for school again, I had to start a new school. This time it was the old middle school, which was situated about 6 doors down from our house in Broad Street, I think I had to go to this school as I was very naughty in my previous school, and they couldn't put up with me anymore. The school in Broad Street was in an old Victorian building, it was built in red brick and it had a tall pointed roof with a weather Vane on top. It was an all girls school and quite a lot of girls went there, when I was in there I made friends with an Indian girl called "Lanaki ". She came from a large Indian family who lived further up Broad Street, her mother and father used to run a Stall in Ely market. I knew they were Indian because her father always used to wear a turban on his head. I would always go around hers a couple of times a week and her family would always make me feel welcome, when I went round hers I always found it weird as they did not have any chairs to sit on, we would sit on cushions on the floor. Sometimes when I was around there her mother would plat my hair and put beads in it, and I would look like a little Indian girl. Also when I went around there I would be able to sample Indian cooking, I used to have this doughy bread called Naan Bread. I also got to try curry for the first time; it was miles to hot and spicy for me, as my stomach was not really used to things like that. Down the bottom of Broad Street there used to be an old fashioned grocery shop, it was painted dark green and had lots of old fashioned metal signs on it. The shop was run by an old widow called Mrs. Dobson I think, her husband probably died during the war.

 She was a friendly chubby lady with grey curly hair, and glasses. She had a son called Andy and he used to work away as a builder. Poor Mrs. Dobson pretty much had to run the shop herself, although sometimes her man friend would come around and do some of the heavy work. The man friend of hers used to go around to all the schools in his car towing a trailer, he would pick up all the left over's from all the school dinners and sell them to the local pig farmers. I will always remember him, as he was a big fat man who was slightly bald and always had a fag in his mouth. Mrs. Dobson was very friendly to our mum and they would always be chatting, sometimes mum would come home from her shop with a big bag of out of date cakes and bread. Mrs. Dobson done this for Mum as she knew Mum struggled to make ends meet. One day

Learn to Love Not Hate

my sister Diane went in there to get something or other, |Mrs. Dobson gave Diane a bag to give to Mum of out of date cakes, but Diane had other ideas. Diane got the bag and walked past Mums house right into the park; she then sat on the swings and ate all the cakes herself. Mum went into the shop the next day and Mrs. Dobson asked Mum if she enjoyed the cakes, she gave to Diane to give to her. My Mum said "what cakes? "And then she laughed. If it was me who done that and not Diane I would have got a severe hiding. Just down the road from No 70 Broad street lived Owens friends, they were called Graham Wade and Gordy Butcher; they lived next door to each other. Gordy Butcher and his mother lived with their Grandparents, as his Mum and Dad had separated. Gordy's Gran was a thin wiry lady who had grey hair; she used to go into Mrs. Dobson's shop to buy her Woodbine cigarettes. One day when I was in the shop I overheard Gordy's Gran talking to Mrs. Dobson about her Daughter (Gordy's Mum) going out with those Yanks again, and this time they had dumped her naked in the middle of the country side. She was telling Mrs. Dobson how she wished her daughter would grow up and sort herself out and stop messing about with the American soldiers. Gordy's Grandparents really spoiled him, as he was a little fat boy. He would get everything he ever wanted and if he didn't he would shout the place down. Graham Wade lived with his parents who both worked very hard and very long hours.

His mum was a cleaner and also worked in the local café, and his dad was a long distance lorry driver. Graham also had an older sister who was Rep of a large firm, because of this Graham was left in the house by himself quite a lot. Sometimes me and my brother would go around there and keep him company, on one occasion we went round there we took cushions and bed sheets down the bottom of the garden and pretended we were camping, we started to light a fire, we lit it using matches Graham had pinched from the kitchen. We then got an old tin and tried to make some drinking chocolate, it turned out to be a really big sticky mess. But at least we thought it was alright, some afternoons I would sit in Grahams kitchen watching his older sister put on her make up as she was getting ready to go out. She was about 20 very grown up and had her own car. Graham's sister was a very pretty girl, and had a steady boyfriend. One day when me and Owen went around there we knocked on the door, and a very unhappy father opened it, he told us we could not see Graham today. We thought something bad had happened as it was very unusual to see Grahams father there. I later learnt that Graham's sister had died in a car accident, her car had stalled half way across a railway crossing, and the train hit her. It was a very sad ending for her and it changed her family's life forever. Graham's mother suffered from a really bad nervous breakdown, and his father had to give up work, to stay at home and look after Graham and her. One of my favorite places to play was on top of Cherry Hill; it was in the park near our house and overlooked the cathedral. The park was full of old oak trees which we would climb up, The Park also had a lot of cows in it, we used to climb to the top of Cherry Hill, and then we would lie on our backs and roll down. We would roll to the bottom and try to stand up, this was very difficult as we were very dizzy. One day when we were rolling down the hill, Owen had his friends Graham's pen knife in his pocket, as he rolled down the hill the pen knife had come open in his pocket and had stuck into his thigh. We had to pull the knife out and then we had to carry him home to our mother. We were worried as it wouldn't stop bleeding, Mum had to take him to the Doctors in Ely, Owen had his first lot of stitches, it was a good job it was Owen and not me, as if it was me my Mum would have called me stupid and shouted at me.

    On one hot and sunny day we went up to Cherry Hill, to play our rolling game, this time we took our youngest brother Robert with us, who lived with Granny and Granddad Lyles at the time, when we got to the top of Cherry Hill Robert was first to go. We watched him roll down the hill and looked in horror as he stood up; he was covered from head to toe in cow muck. The only thing we could do was to take him back to Granny's. She was absolutely livid when she saw him, she then grabbed Robert and took him to our mothers, when she saw our mother she said in no uncertain terms "You had Better Get Him Clean, I Am Not Messing My Bathroom Up." my Mum then went to the shed moaning and groaning and got out the old tin bath. (We didn't have a bathroom at the time), she then filled the old bath with boiling water. While this was cooling down, she took all Roberts clothes off, and then put them in the bath and washed them. She then put Robert in the bath and scrubbed him until he was clean. She then took Robert out the bath and dressed him in some of Owens old clothes. She then took him back to Granny's with a little bag of wet clothes, she was very angry that this had messed up her day. When Owen, Diane and me finally got home that afternoon, mum was still in a foul mood, she grabbed hold of us as we walked in the room and gave us a really big hiding. She then sent us all to bed, with nothing to eat.

On other occasions we would go down to Granny's and unlock the back gate with a hair grip, after we had eventually unlocked the back gate we would then call out Roberts name and tell him to come and play with us. Me, Owen and Diane would then take him down to the river and we would play on to the old chain driven ferry, which was moored near a pub called the' Cutter and the Quay ' we were jumping on and off the ferry when Robert lost his footing and fell in the river. We panicked and started shouting, after a lot of shouting, and tugging and pulling, Owen managed to get Robert out of the River, Robert stood out on the river bank crying his eyes out, as the water was dripping off him. It was coming out of his sleeves and pockets and running out of his shorts. We didn't know what to do, and then we had an idea of taking him to the toilets in the boathouse. We then tried to dry him with towels and bits of toilet paper, we done the best we could and then we took him home. He was still slightly damp (soaking wet). We reached Granny's house crept around the back gate and pushed Robert through it, and then we scampered off. I didn't know what Granny thought when she saw Robert, but I guess she thought it had something to do with us three, but she couldn't prove it. After that incident a big bolt was put on the back gate which was Valerie proof. At my school in Broad Street they used to open it on Sundays, in the mornings they held Sunday school in the big assembly hall.

They used to teach us about the good and evil, and about God and the Devil. I think the Devil made a big impression on me as I was scared stiff of him. In the afternoon after they had given us a glass of squash and a sandwich, they would let us play records on the old wind up Gramophone. We would sing along and do a bit of dancing. We used to enjoy this a lot, and we would go home and to bed happy, ready for another week to start. I don't remember a lot about that school but I remember one incident that had stuck in my mind. One day I was making a lot of noise in the classroom and the teacher whose name was

Mrs. Burnett, took me by the arm and locked me in the big cupboard, and said "Perhaps that will teach you to be quiet, Valerie." what she forgot is that she had a box of chocolates in the cupboard she got for her birthday. I found them and sat on the floor and ate the lot apart from the soft ones (I didn't like them ones), that kept me quiet. Mrs. Burnett was usually a nice teacher; she was very pretty and lived alone in Broad Street, after her husband left her. One day at school in the Biology lesson, one of the boys brought in a dead grass snake. When the teacher got it out the box, I nearly fainted and went screaming into the toilets, I missed the rest of the lesson. When we were there something really scary happened, Diane and I were playing in the Cul De Sac, in Broad Street near a house where a retired Vicar lived with his wife. He suffered from senile dementure, He came out of his house and asked Diane and me could if he could put his hands down our knickers, I immediately said " No" but Diane was lagging behind me, she must have said "Yes" because when I looked back I saw her running from behind a fence screaming her head off, with the old Vicar chasing behind her. As that happened the Vicars wife came out the house and dragged him in doors. That evening the police came round and interviewed us, I don't know what happened to him but we never heard any more about it. It was late October at No 70 Broad street and Owen, Diane and me were still surviving with our mum. Our house did not have any electric mains to it, although a lot of houses in Broad Street had electric by this time, but our mother could not afford to have it put on.

We still relied on gas to light the old portal lamps; we cooked on an old wood burning Rayburn, which also heated the hot water. This was to old fashioned and she decided to have electric put in the house. She decided we would have to get some extra money from somewhere, so she arranged with Mr. Burton, the local farmer, that we would all go potato picking and he was very happy with this. Mum took us Off School during the week. Monday morning came and we were up bright and early, it had been raining all the previous week but today was really cold and frosty. We wrapped up well, got our flasks and sandwiches and headed off to the Burtons Farm. We had to go up Cherry Hill, and cut through an old building that was owned by the Kings School. When we eventually reached the Burtons farm, we had

Learn to Love Not Hate

to get a lift to the potato field on a trailer which was pulled by an old grey Massey Ferguson tractor. So Mum, Diane, Owen and Me jumped on the trailer with a load of old men and women who were also going potato picking. We finally reached the potato field after a long and bumpy trip; we were shown to our place on the field which was marked by two sticks.

We were given a basket each and told to pick the potatoes in between our sticks, after the potato spinner had been down the field. A potato spinner was a big wheel on the back of a tractor, which dug the potatoes out of the ground. Mum and us then had to rummage though the dirt, to find the potatoes that had been dug out, this was really back breaking work. When the basket was full Owen would tell me to go and empty it into a trailer at the end of the field, after a hard morning's work the tractor driver would stop for his dinner and us potato pickers would head towards the big hedge on the side of the field, to take shelter from the wind. We settled down to eat our sandwiches we had taken with us and a nice cup of tea out of our flasks. In the afternoon after our lunch break we carried on with our picking. As the afternoon wore on, one of the old men picking behind us noticed Owen making me carry the basket to the trailer and he shouted out to Owen "Give the girl a rest and you carry the baskets to the trailer, you lazy little bugger." the old man must have really scared Owen, as he took the baskets to the trailer the rest of the afternoon.

In fact he carried the baskets to the trailer for the rest of the week. We really enjoyed the potato picking that week, although it was cold and wet and back breaking. This was one of the only things we done as a whole family, I don't think the money we earned went towards putting the electric in the house. During the last few months of living in Broad street mum had met a local farmer, called Herbert Johnson and he owned his own farm and he was quite well off. Herbert was 25 years older than Mum, soon after Mum and Herbert got together, Mum fell pregnant, and along came little brother 'Bert'. Not long after Bert was born Mum fell pregnant again and Herbert decided it was time to make an honest women of her. So on one cold winter's morning, Mum got dressed in her best winters cloths and walked up to Ely register office and got married to Herbert, it was a really quite wedding. They were the only ones there apart from a couple of witnesses, after the wedding ceremony they all went down the local pub and celebrated over a couple of drinks, there was no big reception. One Saturday at the house my mother asked my step dad Herbert to take my sister Diane up to the shoe shop in Ely, and buy her a new pair of shoes for school. I got upset when I heard this as I looked after my clothes and I never got any new shoes. I got upset over this and went storming out the back door, screaming and shouting my head off. I ran outside and locked myself in the old backyard toilet. Mum and Herbert stood outside the toilet trying to get me out, I kept saying " NO ", not until you get me some new shoes.

Mum had enough of all of this and said stay in there then you little Cow!!, after what seemed like a long while mum had gone inside shouting and swearing, when it had all died down Herbert came up with idea of throwing a bucket of water over the door, into the toilet. So Herbert found a bucket of ice cold water, and threw it over the top of the door. This caused me to start screaming and shouting again, after a while Granny Lyles who lived next door had heard all the screaming and she came round to see what all the noise was about. Mum told her what was going on and Granny Lyles came to the toilet door and said "Come on out Valerie, I will get you some new shoes," I slowly appeared out the toilet door. I was cold and dripping wet and said "Hello, Granny," and then I went inside and got changed. The next day a pair of grotesque looking blue sandals appeared round our house, they were standing on the hall table with a note attached to them, which read:

"To,
Valerie as Promised
Love from Granny Lyles. "

I wore them horrible shoes the whole of the school term, I couldn't really say "No," after all the fuss I had made, come to think of it, those horrible sandals must have been indestructible, as I remember Owen wearing them the whole of the next school term.

Learn to Love Not Hate

I remember one winters evening just before Christmas, Diane and me saw our real Dad cycling up Broad Street on his bike, with the old gas lights on the back beaming brightly. He was working for the railway, and he had cycled from Little Downham to Ely, he had seen us and he stopped. He asked us would we like to go to the pantomime in London. Which his railway social club were organizing for Christmas, we said "Yes "if our mum agreed. So we walked with him down the road to our house. My Dad

Knocked on the door and my Mum appeared, my dad asked about the trip and she agreed, she was probably glad to get rid of us. So on one frosty morning just after Christmas my Father, Owen, Diane and Me were waiting by the side of the road, waiting for the bus to turn up. The bus arrived after a short while and we got on and sat down, with a big bag of sweets.

Then we started the long journey to London. After what seemed like hours on the bus, we arrived at the Big City, we got off the bus and went and found something to eat, as it was dinner time. After a lovely dinner, our father took us to a large toy shop. Then he brought us a little Christmas present. I can't remember what he got us but at least it was something, then it was time to make our way to the theatre in the West end, for the afternoon matinee of Wind in the Willows, we sat there amazed at the life sized animals. Who were dancing and singing on the stage, Dad then brought us an ice cream in the interval. When it was all over we left the theatre dancing and singing, we were really happy. We had never seen nothing like that before in our lives, we then boarded the bus that was waiting for us. Then we headed out of the bright lights of London, on the journey back home. We got back to Ely and said our thanks and goodbyes; we then happily went to bed and dreamed of giant Toads and Giant mice.

Chapter 16
.After Mum Remarried.

After mum was remarried to Herbert things changed a little bit for the better, Herbert was quite well off as he had his own farm, so he had a little bit of money. Because of this Owen, Diane and I started to get a little bit of pocket money. We had never had pocket money before in our short lives. On Saturdays I used to wake up early, and cross the road to an old lady who used to live almost opposite to us. She would always give me a cheerful smile and tell me to come in for a cup of tea and a biscuit. While I drunk my tea, she would get her shopping list ready. After I had drunk my tea, I would go down the road to old Mrs. Dobson's and any other shop I needed to go, so I could get all the shopping on the old ladies shopping list. When I had finished the shopping I would struggle back to the old ladies house loaded with the bags, she was ever so pleased and showed her appreciation by giving me 5 shillings, which was quite a lot of money in those days.

I would then go over the road towards our house. When I got home my mother and Herbert had just had their breakfast, mum would then call Owen, Diane and me and give us our pocket money of (10p) each. When dinner time came Mum and Herbert would get ready to go for a drink. Mum would then say her farewells and send us out of the house, as she used to lock all the doors and shut all the windows. She didn't care what we got up to as long as we were out the way, baby Bert would go around Nanny and Granddad Lyles with our other brother Robert. After Mum and Herbert had gone, me, Diane and Owen would head

Learn to Love Not Hate

up to Ely town centre. Our first port of call would be the fish' n' chip shop, where my Mum would do some part time cleaning. Because mum worked there the owner of the shop would let us have a portion of chips for half price, we used to get them for three old pennies about (1 and a half p) instead of a sixpence (2 and a half p). We would then sit on the bench on the edge of the market and eat our chips, and watch the people go by. There were a lot of characters in those days. When the chimes hit 2'o'clock on the old bells, we would head towards 1 of the 2 picture places located near the market. There was a posh one called the "Rex "which used to cost 1 shilling and a sixpence (7 and a half p), to get in and a cheaper one , affectingly known as the "fleapit" which used to cost (5p) to get in. we would always try to get into the fleapit so we could save sixpence, but sometimes we would have to go to the Rex if the fleapit was only showing films for adults. It didn't mean much to me as the Rex always showed better movies anyway, I remember watching fondly " South Pacific", and " Seven brides for Seven Sons" with one of my favorite actors Howard Keel in it.

I also remember seeing "Summer Holidays" and "The Little White Bull" starring Tommy Steele. When we were in the Rex we would sneak into the cloak room where the people would hang their coats, we would then go though the pockets. When the film had finished and the people started to leave, we would kneel down behind the seats, when we were knelt down we would crawl along the rows looking for dropped sweets and anything else people had dropped on the floor, sometimes we were lucky sometimes we were not. After a while a new lot people would start coming in we would stand up and take our seats again and sit though the same film again. We had to do this because we couldn't go home until out parents came back from the pub, which was usually around 8'o'clock at night, when the film had finished we left the cinema and had to walk home all the way back to our house, down all the dark streets all by ourselves.

This was quite scary as there were quite a lot of unsavory people starting to gather as it was Saturday night. There were a lot of Mods and Rockers and Gypsies about. We knocked on the door and our step father Herbert would answer the door, Mum was never there she always stayed down the pub till closing time. When we got home Herbert would sit us down and made sure we had a cup of tea and a slice of bread with some cheese, Herbert wasn't such a bad man he looked after us pretty well. After we had eaten our food it would be near 9'o'clock and time for bed, the rest of the week bedtime would be 7'o'clock. This was for Mums and Herbert's benefit. Some afternoons after school we would head , in to Ely town centre and we used to go to a shop called 'Peacocks', we would walk around Peacocks, pretending to look around, and then when the person behind the counter went out the back, we would stuff our pockets with pencils, crayons and anything else we could fit in. We would then disappear before the shop assistant returned. Diane who was always with us, must have taken this in, as a week later Diane went in Woolworths by herself, she picked up a carrier bag and filled it up with anything she liked, including a pretty little doll, she then walked out the store and nobody stopped her, although somebody must have seen her, recognized her and reported her. Later on that night a police car pulled up outside our house, and two big policemen got out and knocked on the door.

Mum answered the door and invited them in. the older of the two policemen told Mum what Diane had been up to that afternoon. Mum then called Diane downstairs and the big policeman gave her a right good telling off. This really scared Diane as she ran upstairs crying her eyes out, nothing else was done about it and the bag was returned to Woolworths. She probably got away with this because of her age, as she was only 8 years old. Mum didn't even say anything, if it was me I would probably have got a good hiding. One of granny Lyle's old school friends called Stanley used to sweep Broad Street at least once a week, because Granny knew him, Mum became friendly with him as well. When he was sweeping next to our house, Mum would take him out a cup of tea, and a couple of biscuits, Stanley would sit on the streets and enjoy his cup of tea and biscuits, when he had finished he returned the cup back to mum, he would say thank you then he would carry on with his sweeping. Stanley the road sweeper used to live in an old railway carriage down by the allotments. One day Stanley fell seriously ill with a bad illness, and he had to go to hospital. Granny Lyles and my mother went to visit him sometimes. After he had been in hospital for quite a long while, Stanley started to get better.

The welfare people asked Stanley where he lived, Stanley told them and they went to inspect his place. They came back to the hospital and

Learn to Love Not Hate

told Stanley that he could not go back there, as it was too cold and too damp for him to live in. They also told him he needed someone to keep an eye on him. The welfare people knew that Granny Lyles was friends with Stanley, so they went round to visit Granny and asked if she could help out. She said she couldn't do anything for Stanley but she knew someone who could. Granny Lyles then came round to Mums, and asked Mum if she could put Stanley up in the spare room she had. My mother then started to come up with all sorts of excuses, until Granny mentioned the welfare would pay Mum rent to look after Stanley. Mum then made her mind up straight away, for the next couple of days mum was busy tidying and cleaning the spare bedroom. The spare room was a state as it hasn't been used in years. I had never seen Mum work so hard, it's amazing what a bit of money can make people do, Stanley then moved in the following Monday. Where he got better and better, Stanley stayed at our house for about 6 months until one night he had a relapse and died in his bed. Mum found him when she took his breakfast up for him. Mum called the Doctor, and then the ambulance took him away, and that was the end of Mums little earner. A couple of weeks after Stanley had passed away Mum said to me," Valerie it's a shame to waste that spare bedroom, I think it is about time you had your own bedroom."

I think she done this, to break me and Diane up. I moved my stuff into the spare bedroom but I couldn't settle, and I didn't get any sleep I used to have terrible nightmares in that room. Some nights I used to wake up screaming, thinking I had seen Stanley sweeping the bedroom floor. After a whole week of me screaming and shouting, Mum couldn't put up with it anymore, I was quickly moved back with Diane. While Stanley was staying with us Me, Owen and Diane used to go down the allotments and play in Stanley's old railway carriage, but when Stanley died this all came to an end, as the welfare came and removed all of his belongings and then they burnt down the old carriage. Until there was nothing left of where Stanley lived. On one occasion Me, Owen and Diane where walking down the street and came across on the floor a 10 shillings note (50p). So I quickly kneeled down picked up the note and slipped it in my pocket. I then looked around to make sure no one had noticed, we then trotted away. One of our favourite games we used to play was Doctors and Nurses, but we never had any bandages or things to use. I decided that because I had some extra money, I would go to the chemist and buy some medical supplies. I brought a load of bandages, plaster safety pins and I managed to get some Aspro tablets, they used let children buy things like that in those days. When I got home we started to play Doctors and Nurses and I was the patient.

Doctor Owen and Nurse Diane started to treat my pretend broken arm, and gave me a handful of Aspro tablets to take. I unknowingly swallowed them with a cup of water. I must have overdosed on them because a little while later I started to go loopy. I started to run around the bedroom pulling the bed to bits and pulling down the curtains. My step Dad heard all the noise and came upstairs to see what was going on. Mum wasn't there she was out as usual, Herbert got hold of me and made me sit next to Owen as he tidied the bedroom and put the curtains back up. , he gave me a glass of water and tucked me up in bed in bed, I kept getting out and Herbert had to keep tucking me back in. Eventually after a long while I nodded off, Herbert didn't have a clue what I had taken, I was very lucky I woke up in the morning and Doctor Owen and Nurse Diane didn't need to be called. Also during the school holidays Owen, Diane and Me had to find things to do, to occupy ourselves.

Some days when the weather was nice, we would walk up to Ely and go and play near the cathedral. We would sit on the grass and watch all the American tourists, with their expensive clothes and taking photographs, with their expensive cameras. There used to be tourists from all over the world, the Japanese used to make us laugh with their funny eyes and their big teeth. You didn't have to pay admission to get in the cathedral in those days. So we would go in to the cathedral and see what we could get up to, the main aisle of the cathedral had wings which were devoted entirely towards women, it was a place where women and girls could go and pray. I always used to say prayers when I was in there to apologize for being naughty. I must have said a lot of prayers. We would also go and play on the big cannon, which stood on the green outside the cathedral. It was ever so big to us, it seemed like it was 10 feet tall. Just down the road from cathedral was a spooky old Victorian building called the ' Palace school ', which used to be a nursing home, for wounded soldiers in the second world war. But now

Learn to Love Not Hate

it had become a boarding school, for children who suffered from the drug Thalidomide.

I was always told by our mother that the palace school was haunted by an old Nurse, who had died there during the Second World War. It was said you could see her walking up and down the staircases carrying a lamp. I used to scare Owen and Diane by saying to them "LOOK, there goes the old Nurse with her lamp, past the window up there." they used to look and then I would say "No the other window down there," this used to go on until they had really believed they had seen the ghost. Towards the end of the summer holidays, at the beginning of September, we would head up to Cherry Hill Park while the dew was on the ground and an eerie mist hung on the top of the hill. We would be carrying some paper bags; we had got off Mrs Dobson the shopkeeper. When we got to the top of the Hill we would then hunt for a decent blackberry bush. We would then set about picking the big juicy blackberries, with Owen and Diane moaning about getting pricked by the thorns. After we had been picking them all morning and our arms would be bleeding from all the thorns and our hands bright red from all the juice, we had filled all our bags with blackberries. We then began our journey back to Broad Street feeling a bit sick from black berries we had eaten.

After we had been home, and washed our hands and had a cup of tea. We had a slice of bread with jam; we would then go out again. After picking up our bags of blackberries, which we had hid in the back garden, away from the prying eyes of our Mum. We would then go up and down Broad Street knocking on all the old women's doors; we would ask them if they wanted to buy any blackberries. We used to charge 3 pennies (1 and a half p) for a bag. They would jump at the chance to buy some as this meant it would save them from staining their hands and getting cut by the thorns and also wasting a whole afternoon picking them. It didn't take long to sell out but sometimes we would save a bag to take home to our mother, just on the off chance she would be in a good mood. If she was in a good mood, she would make our step father and us some black berry pies, we never told her about the money we made. We would hide that up for some sweets for the weekend. On Sunday mornings when we got up we would, look out through the bedroom window and see what the weather was like. If it was a nice morning we would get dressed, go downstairs and slide out the backdoor. Mum and Herbert never got up on Sunday mornings. It was early as we walked up the deserted street and on the way to Ely city centre, and up to the old market, where they used to hold dances on a Saturday night for women and men. Owen, Diane and Me then started looking about, we would look up all the side streets and also rummage through all the bins.

We would be looking for money which had been dropped or anything else that could be considered useful. We searched for ages not having any luck. Then we came across a rubbish bin that was stuffed full, we started pulling all the rubbish out, and came across a pair of silk stockings. God knows what they were doing there, anyway me and Diane sat on a bench and started to try them on, to see what it was like to be grown up. While we were trying the stockings on an old lady who was an old friend of our mothers, came up to us and said "Take them Bloody Dirty things off, before you catch something." We quickly took them off and threw them back in the bin, and scampered off hoping the old lady would not tell our mother. When the holidays were over and it was time for school again, I had finished at the school at Broad Street and I had to move to a new school in Silver Street. Silver street school which was situated at the back of St Mary's next to Oliver Cromwell's house in the middle of Ely. Silver Street was a school which took both boys and girls but we had our lessons and playtime separate. We had separate class rooms in different halves of the school and the playground was split down the middle by a big fence. My brother Owen had already been at Silver Street for a whole term, Owen and I used to walk to school together. This was quite a long way from our house in Broad Street. While we were getting ready for school in the mornings, our stepfather Herbert would make us some sandwiches for dinner which would have dubious fillings, on the way to school Owen and I would throw the sandwiches over the wall or feed then to the ducks on the river, but the ducks would not even eat them. We threw are sandwiches away as we knew we would get a free school dinner, we didn't get on very well at Silver Street, and Owen and I started misbehaving quite badly.

Owen would not read anything, instead of reading the books they gave him; he would sit there reading comics under his desk. Owen used

Learn to Love Not Hate

to have a very kind women teacher who used to like Owen a lot, she was a very nice lady who was disabled with quite a badly deformed arm. Because this teacher liked him, Owen could get away with murder.

But he couldn't fool the headmaster that easily and because of this he used to get the Cane quite a lot. At break times Owen and I would meet at our secret little gap in the fence, and would stand and talk to each other. We did get caught quite a lot by the playground supervisor and got punished for this. When the dinner bell rang at the end of the morning lessons, all the girls who were going for school dinners would form a line and we would walk down the road to an old Victorian building whilst being supervised by a teacher. When we got there we would all sit down at a big wooden table, and we would be served a basic dinner. It was not too bad, and it was certainly better then the sandwiches Herbert had made for us. After dinner we would walk back to school and begin the afternoon lessons. I didn't have many friends at Silver Street, and was always fighting with somebody in the playground, or on the way home, even on rare occasions in the classroom. This was something I was always getting in trouble for.

When you got in trouble at Silver Street, you were punished by being given jobs to do that were not very nice. One of the jobs you were given was being milk monitor, this job involved going to the back of the school and picking up a crate of milk bottles. The crates used to hold about 30 bottles, the bottles were half a pint big, we would then struggle back to the classroom, when we got in the classroom we had to hand a bottle to everyone in the room. After the lesson had finished the milk monitor would collect all the bottles back up, and put them in the crate. Then we would take the milk crate back to the kitchen, and rinse all the bottles out, and then when the crate was full we would have to carry it to the backdoor and leave it for the milkman to collect.

Another punishment was being ink monitor which was dirtier and more tedious than being milk monitor. This job involved getting a big bottle of ink, from the store cupboard. Then we had to go round and fill up all the ink wells in the desks, the ink wells were little pots the same size as egg cups. This was a very monotonous job, as there were 25 or 30 desks in the classroom. The ink monitor would usually end up with blue hands and blue splash marks on their clothes. When they got home the ink monitor would usually get a smack round the ear for getting ink on their clothes. The pens we had to use had metal nibs, and long wooden handles which we used to dip in the ink wells and write with. When the teacher wasn't looking we used to draw targets on the desk, and play darts with the pens. We would always be asking the teacher for new nibs for our pens, the teachers would always moan and tell us not to press to hard on the pens. Sometimes we would run out of nibs and have to use pencils. This was a punishment as we had to copy all our work out again into our books when we got some nibs.

CHAPTER 17
.GOOD AND BAD TIMES AT THE BANK.

In 1960 after Owen, Diane and myself came out the Nursing home, my father got permission to take us down the bank in Little Downham, to stay with our Aunt Emmy and him. She lived next to the pumping station, Aunt Emmy used to look after the pumping station she was the key holder and she used to get a big rake and pull the weeds out of the filters and, generally keep the place clean and tidy. Aunt Emmy was a spinster and never got married. She once had a boyfriend but she lost him during the war, and she never showed any interest in anyone else. She stayed at home and looked after her mother and father. Aunt Emmy had a little dog called 'Wilby ', she made a lot of fuss of him as he was the only companion she had, for long periods of time. Us three would go down there on our school holidays, Granddad would come and pick us up in his little black Austin car. There was no proper road just a cart track. He used to drive us right along the top of the bank, right next to the river. It used to scare the life out of me, but I trusted Granddad as he was a very good driver. There used to be a lot of cows beside the river, I wasn't too happy about them either. Aunt Emmy was a well built lady who was very tall and she also wore glasses and a little bobble hat.

Her hair was long and pinned and she wore it under her hat, she was about 50 years old when I started going to see her. She was a very caring and nice lady, as she also made sure we never went hungry. She used to have an old rayburn cooker in the kitchen in which she used to cook massive Yorkshire puddings which were really crispy, she also used to cook wild geese my dad would have shot, down on the wash. Aunt Emmys parents lived in a bungalow right near the pumping station, it had orchards all around it and they consisted of apple and plum trees, she used to cook the apples and plums when they were in season and make wonderful pies. One of my favorite memories was when I was 10 years old. I was sitting on an old wooden chair, with a big Pyrex bowl full of evaporated milk, butter and icing sugar. I was whipping it up to make cream for the cream horns of which we all loved. It took ages to get the cream whipped, and my arms were really aching. I recall in the middle of summer I went into the scullery, to make myself lemonade. In those days we used to get the lemonade powder in a tin, I made myself a lemonade and drunk it.

Little did I know Aunt Emmy had stored some weed killer in that tin. Aunt Emmy saw me drinking the lemonade and asked where I had got it from. I told her I got it out the tin, my Aunt and Dad went crazy because they thought I had poisoned myself. They sat me in a sink and made me drink loads and loads of salty water, to try and make me sick. I was eventually sick and that made them happy, I must have been alright as I am still here today. I used to love being in her old bungalow, as it was filled with old pictures and old clocks. They seemed to be chiming everywhere. At night we used to sit around the big wooden table under the old Tilley lights. We sat quietly listening to the radio; we used to love listening to 'Dick Barton', the detective. We used to also play card games and dice games; we used to have Tilley lights and candles as they never had electricity down on the bank. I remember I was sitting near the Rayburn oven on an old chair whilst Dad was telling me how it was my Mum's fault that Elwin died.

He was telling me how she would neglect him, he was saying Mum would never change his nappy or looked after him properly.

I think he was telling me this as he wanted me to go and live with him, when I had left school when I became 15. But I was a real Mums girl, as good or bad as she was, I would always stay with her. I remember during the hot summers, Gran and granddad would be sitting in the kitchen, while Owen, Diane and me would be playing in the garden.

Learn to Love Not Hate

At the bottom of the garden, I remember there was an old Anderson Shelter. I remember Aunt Emmy would tell us to never go near it, as it was old and dangerous. It was half underground and had been there since the end of the war. This is when the story starts to get a little bit more serious. One day Dad said to us would you like to go swimming. We all thought this was a fantastic idea as we had never gone swimming in our lives.

I suppose Diane and me went swimming in our knickers and vest and Owen went in his pants, as none of us owned a swim suit. Aunt Emmy gave him some old towels, we took our towels and we must have walked several miles until we got to the part of the river we could swim safely in. When we got there we stripped down and Dad stripped down to his pants and swam with us. We must have had a good time. When it was time to go Dad started to dry Diane and Me with the towel and then he went too far, he put his hand down our knickers and done unmentionable things. I was so upset about what happened but I didn't tell Aunt Emmy or anybody else, next time he asked me if I wanted to go swimming I strictly said no and wouldn't go. Some days we would walk the two miles up the bank with our Dad to visit our Granny and Granddad Winters, who lived on the farm, Granddad was quite well off as he was probably the only person down the bank to have electricity. Which was supplied by a diesel generator, he ran the lights and T.V. off it. Granny Winters was always so loving and caring to us, Granny was a big lady, which I mean chubby, probably around 18 stone. They were always so pleased to see us. Granddad thought the world of me.

He would always put me on his lap, and sometimes he would take me for a ride on his John Deere tractor. Granny taught me how to knit and sew. I remember one summer when I was down there, my father and his brother were having an argument about Dad setting fire to some barns or bales of straw, and Dad ran in the house and got his shotgun. Granddad tried to get the gun off him and Dad threatened him with it. I think Dad was about 29 then, we then returned home to no 70 Broad street after the holidays. After we had been home for a few weeks, I was standing in the scullery with my mother, when she said" You are going back to Aunt Emmys for the Christmas holidays. ", it was then that I told mum that Dad had interfered with me, I told mum

I didn't want to go, but Mum would not listen to any of it. She just told me to tell Aunt Emmy when I got there. So when we got down there for the Christmas holidays I didn't tell Aunt Emmy as I didn't want to upset her, as she might not understand as she was a spinster. Christmas down the bank really was something else, Aunt Emmy would get a massive Christmas tree that reached from the floor to the ceiling, and it was covered in wonderful decorations, chocolates and illuminated with real candles. We would have lots of wonderful festive food. I remember Dad bought me a gold and black singer sewing machine that actually worked and he bought Diane a similar one which was blue, He got Owen a metal Meccano set. We all played happily with our toys, on the big wooden table under the Tilley lamps until it was time to go to bed. My father slept in the front room on a camping bed. Diane and me had our own little room and Owen had a little room down the passage.

In the morning Dad called me to his bedside and he pulled his bed cloths back, then he would tell me to play with him, but I was disgusted and said no. he told me to get close to the bed so I ran away into the kitchen, to be near Aunt Emmy. I don't think he was very pleased, I didn't say anything to Aunt Emmy. A few days later he said he was going to take us to see our Aunt and Uncle, they lived down the bank. We wrapped up well and set off on foot. Our Aunt and Uncle had three sons, they lived in a really nice old fashioned house, with a massive garden. My uncle worked on the land and so did my auntie, they must have lived near to a farm as there was lots of barns and sheds about. We were all walking round the back of the barns when Dad sent Diane and Owen back to our Auntie, he then took me into the barn, took my knickers off me and inserted his fingers, I asked him what he was doing, he said was doing this to make sure our step father Herbert was not interfering with me. I told him to stop as he was hurting me, he then told me to put my knickers on and we went to our Aunties as if nothing had happened.

We then had tea and a chat and after that we walked back, not much was said on the way back, as I was terribly upset. A few days later we returned back to our mother in Broad Street as the Christmas holidays were over. I didn't tell Mum what had happened as she didn't care before when I told her. About six months later Dad had us back down the bank as it was the school holidays, I went as it done no good protesting. It all seemed strange down there this time. There was a strange atmosphere around Granny and Granddad but Aunt Emmy was alright though, little did we know this would be the last time we could go down there for three years. Dad had arranged with my Auntie to perm my hair as a surprise, we had a really lovely summer there. A few weeks later I found out they had sent Dad to prison for raping a young local girl. He was sent to prison for about three years, Granny and Granddad tried to set up meetings but our Mum said no, as prison was no place for children. I didn't see my father until 1966, those were the Good and Bad times at the bank.

Chapter 18 (Part One)
.Summer at Aunt Nell's.

I recall at the start of the summer holidays in 1960 when I was 10, Diane and I went to stay for a week at our Aunt Nell's in Cherry Hinton near Cambridge, we got up early on the Saturday morning, and happily packed our suit cases and went downstairs, we stood our suit cases in the hall and we went into the kitchen and sat at the kitchen table and had some toast for our breakfast before our long journey to Cherry Hinton. When the time came to leave, we sat down of the table and said our goodbyes to our mother and our little brother Owen, we then picked up our suit cases and made our way to the bus stop, when we got there we waited patiently for the bus to Cambridge. Eventually the coach turned up and Diane and I got on the coach dragging our little suit cases behind us, when we got on the bus we found our seats, and then we settled down for the hour long journey to Cambridge.

After a short while the conductor came around and we paid him our fare, after a long journey the bus pulled in to Cambridge bus station. We were met at the bus station by a wrinkly old lady, who was very short at 5 feet tall she was also accompanied by another old lady. Who was about 90 and was also about the same age, according to our mum. The smaller of the two old ladies came up to us and said "Hello you must be Valerie and Diane." I am your aunt Nell and this is my friend Joyce, who lives with me. Joyce was a little bit older then Nell, who was strict looking and wore thick framed glasses. Aunt Nell gave us a kiss and a cuddle each, and then took us for a cake and a cup of tea at the

Learn to Love Not Hate

bus station. We really liked that, as we were dry and hungry after our journey. After our tea and cakes, aunt Nell and Joyce took us to find a taxi for a short journey into Cherry Hinton, we got into the taxi and after a short journey we arrived at aunt Nell's house.

Diane and I was amazed at what we had saw, aunt Nell's place was massive, we had never seen nothing like it before, it looked like something out of a fairy tale, it had pure white plastered walls, it also had loads of windows all with little diamonds shaped panes in them, and a big rivet studded front door, the big roof was covered in straw, and yet more windows embedded in the straw. The front garden had a big lawn and also had a big willow tree, with flower borders which contained nearly every colour of the rainbow. And there was climbing roses climbing up the bright white walls, we all got out of the taxi and me and Diane followed Aunt Nell and Joyce up the path to the front door. Aunt Nell unlocked the door and we entered the house. We then went into the hallway. Diane and I stood there amazed, the hall had pictures hanging from every wall, and the floor was covered with nice red carpet. In one corner there was an antique table, and in another corner there was a coat stand, and right at the end of the hall stood an enormous grandfather clock. Aunt Nell lead us into the kitchen, and sat us at a big oak table and made us some jam sandwiches, with big thick slices of crusty bread, while Aunt Nell made the sandwiches we had a look around, and there were was more pictures on the walls and against one of the walls there was a enormous welsh dresser, which displayed lots of antique plates and cups. Above the sink was an old fashioned water heater known as a geezer, which hissed and banged every time Aunt Nell turned the hot Water tap on, this made Diane and me giggle. After we had eaten our sandwiches Aunt Nell walked to the corner of the room and turned on this big plastic box, it turned out to be a television. Me and Diane sat there with our eyes wide open we had never watched a television very often, we watched Muffin the Mule, then we watched the news with Aunt Nell and Joyce, the news was followed by Saturday night at the London palladium.

When it had finished it was time for bed, Aunt Nell made us a cup of cocoa and after we had drunk that she led us up the big oak stairs to our bedrooms, Aunt Nell opened the door and stood there were two little single beds covered in flowery bedspreads. There were oak beams in the ceiling as the bedrooms were in the roof of the house, Aunt Nell kissed us good night and we got ready for bed. We woke up in the morning got dressed and went to the bathroom to have a wash. When we got out the bathroom we were met by aunt Nell who had just got up. She then led us to the stairs when we got to the stairs she stopped at a picture of a man in a navy uniform, she explained this was picture of her late husband and he was a navy commander, she explained that he travelled a lot in the First world war and that's why the house is full of antiques. She then told us that her husband's ship was sunk during the First World War and he was drowned and after that she never remarried, we then carried on down the stairs and into the kitchen, where her friend Joyce had prepared a breakfast of bacon, egg and toast for us.

We ate this happily and said our thanks, we then got ready to go out, we headed towards the backdoor and looked out. It was drizzling and quiet cold for this time of the year, we then went back and put our coats on. We then headed towards the backdoor and went out in to the garden. Which was full of trees flowers and bushes, we walked towards the bottom of the garden where we discovered a little summer house, it was made of wood with a felt roof, and had a veranda on the front of it, to sit on in the sun. Diane and I went up towards the summer house and approached the big glass doors; we tried the handles and discovered it was unlocked. We went into the summer house and inside of it was just like Aunt Nell's house, there were old Victorian pictures hanging on the wall and a old table with a couple of chairs standing on the old varnished wooden floors, along the end wall we noticed there were three old fashioned Victorian travelling chests Diane and I thought they looked interesting so we went up towards the chest, to see if they were unlocked. To our surprise they were, so we opened them up inside the first one there were loads of old Victorian dresses, all folded up nice and neatly. Inside the second chest there were lots of hats of different sizes and colours packed tidily. Inside the third chest there were loads of shawls and feather boas, and on top them, laid a selection of old Chinese fans. Diane and I thought it would be fun to dress up in those so first of all we, picked a dress each that we liked and put it on, next we picked a couple of hats. Mine had loads of feathers

Learn to Love Not Hate

on it and Diane's was black with a long veil on it, which came down and covered her face.

We finished off with a couple of feathered boas which were so long they came down to the floor, we then picked up an old Chinese fan, and started to fan ourselves. At that moment aunt Nell and her friend Joyce came walking down the garden trying to find us to tell us it was dinner time. They saw us parading up and down the veranda dressed in the Victorian clothes, and Aunt Nell and Joyce nearly wet themselves laughing. Aunt Nell then called out "Come on you little madams, dinner is ready", we then carefully took the clothes off and put them neatly back in the trunks, as we walked back up in the garden Aunt Nell told us they were the clothes she used to wear when she was a young girl and she never got around to getting rid off them as she was a horder, in fact aunt Nell's house was like the Aladdin's cave full of treasures. She never got rid of anything only the kitchen rubbish, we passed the rest of the afternoon after a lovely dinner, reading books and watching the old television, as it was raining quiet heavily by now. The next day when we got up it was still raining and still quiet chilly, after we had breakfast, Aunt Nell said she is going to take us to meet her son, who lived in a bungalow right at the very back of the garden.

Kenneth her son had built it by himself so he could be near his Mum, Kenneth was not married and lived by himself Diane and l put on our coats, and went with Aunt Nell down the Garden Path, past the summer house and then went through a gate in a big prickly fence and there stood Kenneth's bungalow it was just as pretty as aunt Nell's house and it had a lovely garden, we knocked on the door and Kenneth greeted us with a big smile and a grateful welcome. He then asked us in for a cup of tea, we sat down in the kitchen with our cups of tea and a biscuit. We then chatted away all morning, he asked us about our family and how they were keeping he then told us where he worked and how he looked after aunt Nell, and her friend. He done all their garden and odd jobs, as they were too old to do anything heavy we thought he was a really nice man, Diane and me had never meet many nice men before, we then walked back to aunt Nell's house, and that day was nearly over. We had some sandwiches for our tea and had an early night.

We got up the next morning after a lovely sleep and it was still cold and raining, what a summer this was turning out to be. Diane and I were starting to get a bit bored, so we started to get a bit nosey around the kitchen, in one of the cupboards we discovered a large pile of shiny sixpences, we didn't know at the time but aunt Nell saved them for her meter, Diane and I grabbed a handful of sixpences and put them in our pockets. Later on that morning we told aunt Nell we were going out, We put on our coats and headed out towards the main road, and into Cherry Hinton. Cherry Hinton was like a small village on the out skirts of Cambridge. There were one or two shops on a busy high street, Diane and I walked up the high street into the first shop which happened to be sweet shop, we filled up a brown paper bag with a selection of sweets and went up to the counter and paid for them with some of the sixpences, we went outside and ate our sweets happily, after we had finished our sweets we went to the other shop and went in. This shop sold all types of things and we used up the rest of our sixpences. To buy some cute little hair clips, with cute little flowers on them. We also brought a cute little pink comb each.

We then headed home back to the busy road to Aunt Nell's, when we entered the kitchen; we were meet by two stern faced women. Aunt Nell said she had gone to get some sixpences but some were missing, she said that Joyce didn't know where they were and Aunt Nell said the mice couldn't get the lid of the jar. She said this with a laugh, and told us it must have been us, she told us if we ever needed any money in the future all we had to do is ask her, we had expected the worse but nothing had happened at home we would have got a good hiding and sent to bed with no tea. On the fourth day we woke at aunt Nell's to a nice sunny morning, at the least the weather had changed. After breakfast we decided to make the most of it, we decided to go up to the woods which were right near the busy road. We climbed trees and played near the little stream, that ran through the woods, while we was picking some flowers we came across a hedgehog waddling through the under growth with its cute little nose poking from its prickles, Diane took her jumper off and wrapped it around the hedgehog. She then picked it up and we put it in a carrier bag we had found, we then went back to Aunt Nell's pleased with ourselves with the present we had

Learn to Love Not Hate

found Aunt Nell and Joyce. Me and Diane walked proudly into the kitchen and put the carrier bag on the kitchen table.

We took Diane's jumper out of the bag and unwrapped it to reveal the hedgehog, Aunt Nell and Joyce jumped back, in disgust. And said in a loud Voice "Get That Bloody Dirty Thing Out of Here!, It Is Disgusting And Full Of Fleas", Diane quickly picked it up in her jumper and took it out in to the back garden, trust us to upset aunt Nell, near the end of our holiday. On Friday morning we got up and decided to take the hedgehog back to the woods' so we went into the back garden, to look for the hedgehog we hunted around and eventually found it under the steps under the old summer house, we picked it up and this time we put it in a old cardboard box. We then walked up the road back to the woods, we had got about half way there and were walking past a big wooden gate, when out popped two enormous heads, and we jumped back in surprise. We then realized they were horses we had in seen pictures of them in books at school, but had never seen them in real life.

We then got brave and walked up to them and started stroking them, and fed them a handful of grass, their tongues tickled our hands as they ate the grass, the horses turned out to be ever so friendly, after quiet a long time of playing with the horses we said goodbyes to them, and took Mr. Hedgehog back to the woods and said good bye to him as well, then we made our way back to aunt Nell's. When we got back we had our tea and settled down for our last evening we were chatting away and Aunt Nell started to tell us that during the Second World War she used to have evacuated children, who had come up from London to escape the bombing, they used to travel up to stay in her house. She told us how she would pick them up at the railway station, and how sad they would look, standing on the platform, holding their little suitcases in one hand and a card within the other hand with a number on it.

She then told how she would take them home and the first thing she would have to do, was give them a bath and scrub them clean, she would cut their hair to get rid of all the fleas, she told us how she had looked after about ten children during the war time and how they still kept in touch, and sent her birthday cards even though some of them must nearly thirty years old now.

Valerie Ann Hobbs

We sat there and listened to all of this, with utter amazement, the next morning it was time to go home, after a big farewell breakfast Aunt Nell took us in a taxi, they had booked back to the bus station in Cambridge. As we waited for the bus to arrive Aunt Nell and Joyce gave us lots of kisses and cuddles. They also gave us a big bag of sweets each for the journey home and then the bus arrived we said our goodbyes and climbed on the bus with our little suitcases and tears in our eyes, we then waved goodbye through the bus window as the bus pulled out of Cambridge on the journey back to Ely, we never went back to aunt Nell's ever again and didn't see much of aunt Nell until I got married in later years.

Chapter 18 (Part 2)

Towards the end of the summer holidays in 1960, mum got pregnant by her boyfriend Herbert, it was her first child from Herbert and to ease the pressure off Mum. Me, Diane and Owen, were sent for a couple of weeks to Uncle |Bobs and auntie Barbara's house down in Southampton. Uncle Bob and auntie Barbara were very well off, and very posh. Uncle Bob was the manager of a large furniture store in the centre of Southampton. They lived in a very big three storey house in the posh end of town. Uncle Bob and auntie Barbara never had children of their own, on the day we were meant to go to Southampton Owen, Diane and me woke up feeling a bit nervous as we had never met them in our whole lives, and we had never been to Southampton. It seemed to us that Southampton was on the other side of the world, we had to be up very early as uncle Bob had told mum it was a very long drive from Southampton to Ely and back in the same day. We sat in our kitchen in Broad Street eating a light breakfast of toast and a cup of tea, as Mum did not want us to be sick on the long journey. At about 10 o clock a big maroon coloured Jaguar car pulled up outside our house, this must have caused a stir in Broad Street as seeing these posh big cars in our street, was a very rare sight.

Everyone must have thought it must have been the prime minister. The door opened and out stepped a big, tall gingery haired man, who was puffing on a pipe, he knocked on the door, Mum answered and in a posh voice he introduced himself as uncle Bob, by this time auntie Barbara had got out the car and uncle Bob introduced her. Auntie

Barbara was wearing some very posh clothes, her hair was immaculate, and she looked like a young version of Queen Elizabeth. My Mum asked if she would like to come in for a cup of tea. Uncle Bob said "that would be grand, we are very dry after the long journey", Mum led them into the kitchen and introduced them to the three of us. After about an hour they had drunk their tea and ate some sandwiches, Mum had made them and they had a chat, uncle Bob said it was time to leave because he would like to get back before it got dark. We said our goodbyes and uncle Bob picked up our big suitcases which were in the hall, he carried them to his car and put them in the big maroon coloured boot. Owen, Diane and me then got in the back of the car and sat in the seat. It was a very big car and we had plenty of space. It was like sitting on a sofa, uncle turned on the car and he started to drive out of Broad Street, we were waving to our Mum out the back of the window, I don't know if Mum was sad or relieved.

We headed out of Ely and headed onto the London road, this was all strange to us as we had never left the county of Cambridgeshire before. After what seemed like forever we finally entered the out skirts of London and uncle Bob pulled up to a small café. We entered the café, sat down and uncle Bob ordered cups of tea and plates of chips. After we finished our meals auntie Barbara took us to the toilets, where we had a wee and then auntie Barbara made us wash our hands properly, so we would not leave any grease on the car seats, uncle Bob did the same with Owen. This was a sign of things to come, we then got back into the car and continued our journey back to Southampton. We arrived in Southampton around about tea time; we were surprised on how big the place was. As we drove past the ship yards we caught a glimpse of the sea, we continued our journey through the docks until we reached another posh looking street, on both sides of the street there were rows of big elegant houses. They had big sparkly windows and big painted doors. Everywhere looked immaculate; there was no rubbish and no children playing anywhere. It was all so different from Broad Street, we got out of the car and uncle Bob took our suitcases out of the car and led us up the steps to the big house. As we entered the house auntie Barbara made us remove our shoes and then we were made to stand them neatly in the hall way. We were shown into the kitchen, we had never seen a kitchen like this before, it was as big as most houses in

Learn to Love Not Hate

Broad Street and it was spotlessly clean, everything sparkled. We were given some sandwiches and given a glass of lemonade, which was ice cold.

As it had come out of a fridge, we had never seen a fridge before. After we had our tea auntie led us upstairs followed by uncle with the suitcases. She led us to our bedroom and opened the door, we couldn't believe our eyes, and everywhere looked so clean and bright.

It was like the houses we used to see at the cinema, Diane and me shared a bedroom, and Owen had a room to himself. We went into our bedrooms, the beds looked brand new, the sheets were pure white and the floor had nice thick carpets on them. We were then told we would have to have a bath every night. We were shown the bathroom and it looked like an operating theatre, we had our bath using scented soaps and soft flannels, we then dried ourselves with soft big thick towels. After we had our bath Owen went in for his bath, this must had shocked him as he only bathed twice a month. We had learnt that people in Southampton bathed once a day not once a week. After all the baths we were put to bed. Auntie and uncle said their goodnights, we then said our prayers and fell asleep in our big soft beds. The next morning auntie Barbara woke us up, and told us to go into the bathroom for a wash, then she told us to leave the bathroom as we would expect to find it. As we were doing this she opened our suitcases and tried to find some clean clothes, while we were in the bathroom auntie came in and took our clothes away, I said to her they are clean they have only been worn once.

Auntie said to us we would have to wear clean clothes every day. She tuttered at the soap ring we had left on the sink. She then wiped the basin with a clean flannel, after she was satisfied the bathroom was clean, she took us downstairs to breakfast .Uncle Bob was already at the table smoking his pipe, and reading the Sunday paper. He looked up and said "Good morning, I trust you slept well", We all said good morning Uncle Bob, Auntie then sat us at the table and gave us a bowl of cereal while she got on cooking some eggs and bacon. After we had finished our breakfast she sent us to wash our hands, we had now washed our hands twice in under an hour, what on earth is going on we thought to ourselves's. After a while of chatting to ourselves Auntie came in and said "Do you mind keeping the noise down." we didn't understand we were barely whispering, soon after Uncle Bob said come on you kids put your shoes on, we are going to the park. It was a nice sunny day and we headed for the park, and on the way Auntie and Uncle took us into a toy shop. Where he bought Owen a toy boat, Diane a skipping rope and me a Ball. We then continued towards the park and entered it through two big metal gates; while we were there we played on the swings a slide and a big metal roundabout.

After we had finished playing they bought us an ice cream off one of the many ice cream vans in the park. We sat on the grass and ate our big ice cream with a big chocolate flake in it, after we had finished aunt wiped our mouths with a big white handkerchief. We then went to a large pond in the middle of the park; Owen then set about sailing his toy boat, while Diane and me took our shoes and socks off and went off for a paddle, in the shallow end of the pond. After a while of playing in the pond Auntie shouted out "Come on children time to go", we dried our feet and put our shoes and socks back on.

We then headed out the park and straight back towards the house. When we reached the house it was off with the shoes and straight to the bathroom, for yet another wash. God at this rate we would be as shiny as the house. When we came downstairs uncle Bob sat us down in the lounge with some children's books, he got from somewhere and told us to be quiet whilst Auntie rustled up a late dinner. Sometime later Auntie called us into the kitchen for our dinner. We had some meat, potatoes and some vegetables. We found our meat very hard to eat as we never had real meat very often, then it was up to the bathroom (again) and then to bed. The next morning we got up and used the bathroom we went downstairs to be greeted by our Auntie, Uncle |Bob had already left to go to work, so that left Auntie to keep us amused. After we had our breakfast our aunt told us to get ourselves ready to go out. We then went out the house and got into a taxi, and headed into Southampton town centre. First of all we went to some shops and done some grocery shopping. When we were at the shops we kept asking Auntie Questions like "what are those long yellow things? (Bananas), and "what are those big hairy things?" (Coconuts) and so on. She answered the questions for about an hour, you could tell she was getting very annoyed. After we had finished our shopping for groceries we went along a big high street to a shop called 'Woolworths', we told Auntie we had a Woolworths

Learn to Love Not Hate

in Ely she just said "yes dear ", we went into Woolworths and while Auntie was at the counter buying something Diane asked Auntie in a rather loud voice yet another question, Our Auntie then finally lost her temper and told us to be quiet and not to say another word. We then caught a taxi home in silence.

When we arrived home Uncle was there back from work, he was sitting there smoking his pipe, and reading his paper. Auntie then sent us into the room and told him to keep us occupied as she went into the kitchen to cook dinner; she said this in a grumpy voice. After we had eaten our dinner auntie sent us to bed early with a book, and told us we could read before we went to sleep. She had forgotten about sending us to the bathroom. In the morning Auntie asked us if we would like to go down the shops and perhaps see the boats in the yard. Auntie seemed to be in a better mood this morning. As we were getting ready she asked us if anyone of us would like to spend a penny before we leave, I replied "We haven't got any money Auntie", Auntie started to laugh,"No, no. It's what respectable people say when they want to go to the toilet." With that we left the house and walked into Southampton, perhaps she thought this would tire us out and make us quiet, we got our shopping without asking many Questions, and then we went to the docks. Luckily that day there was two big ships moored on the quayside, Aunt then explained to us these ships were just like hotels, and rich people went on holiday on these. They sailed to all different parts of the world on these boats, not very interesting to us so we started to ask some questions.

This must have worn Auntie out, as she said she needed a cup of tea. We then headed to a rather posh restaurant, which the rich people used before they got on the boat. Aunt ordered tea for four, and some rather nice cakes. I tried to impress by asking her could I spend a penny now, she smiled at this and took us to the toilets, while we were in the toilets she couldn't resist telling us to wash our hands. By this time we had left the restaurant it was almost 5 'o' clock, so we went to Uncle Bobs furniture shop which was not that far away. We went into the shop which was enormous and we stood staring at all the posh furniture, we had never seen stuff like this. Uncle Bob was just about to leave off work, so we all walked to the car park together and Uncle drove us home, in the big maroon car. This time we had to put up with smoke from his pipe. As he liked to have a puff on the home from work. We arrived home and after an easy dinner of sandwiches and cake, everybody had an early night as Aunt wasn't feeling very well. At least we got out of having a bath that night. The next morning when we got up Uncle was waiting in the kitchen for us, He told us that Auntie would not be getting up as she was very poorly, he said he would be taking the day off work to look after us.

He stood there smoking his pipe and thinking. He then said we would have to stay in the house as he will have Aunt to look after as well, Aunties headache was probably brought on by having us kids in the house, making a lot of noise, after all she was nearly 40 years old and never had much to do with children although she did have a child later on in life. Uncle Bob sat us in the lounge and put the T.V on for us, he also gave us some colouring books and some crayons which he had bought for us. While we were busy colouring Uncle sat at his desk and done some paperwork. Having kids around never seemed to bother him, probably because he came from a large family but Auntie was an only child. He kept going upstairs at regular intervals to check on Auntie, while he was up; he got us glasses of orange juice and some biscuits. At dinner time he told us to behave while he popped out and got us all fish and chips, when he got back we all sat at the kitchen table and Uncle got the fish and chips out on plates. We didn't eat them out the newspaper like they did back in Ely, but all the same we really enjoyed them. It was a real treat for us, in the afternoon we sat down and Uncle would tell us stories about the war. He told us he used to fly the airplanes, he told us how would fly from the airbase near Cambridge and drop bombs in Germany. He also told us how his airplane was shot down and he had to parachute out, he explained how a parachute was like an umbrella. He then talked about how the German soldiers caught him and put him in a German prison for the rest of the war.

We couldn't believe how badly he was treated; he almost had it as bad as we had it when we were back home with Mum. Then he got in touch with our Mum and told her he was bringing us home the next day as Auntie was not very well. We were then sent to our bedrooms, for an early night as uncle wanted to spend some time with Auntie. Uncle then took us upstairs put us to bed and said "Good Night", he told us to try and get some sleep as we had to be up early, The next morning came around and Uncle got us up and made sure our suitcases were packed properly, he then took them outside and put them in the boot of his car.

When we went downstairs Auntie made the effort to get up and make us some breakfast, she told us she would not be travelling back with us as she was not up to it. After breakfast we said our goodbyes to Auntie and she gave us a big kiss and a cuddle, we got into the car and uncle let me in sit in the front seat as I was the oldest. We then set off and we did not stop at the café, we just had a short stop to "spend a penny". We arrived back in Ely in a record time as uncle wanted to get back to Auntie. He didn't stop round ours for a cup of tea, He just gave us a kiss and said goodbye to Mum. He then shot off in the car; we didn't see auntie and uncle again, although he did send me and Diane a big Dolls house. He had made it by hand and filled it with pieces of furniture for Christmas, we will always remember that.

Chapter 19
.Caught at the Swimming Pool.

During the summer holidays in 1962, while we were at Wilburton special school, the weather was hot, it was the longest holiday of the year and we were looking forward to it. Owen, Diane and I was also looking forward to getting away from all the stupid kids. We wondered what we could do to pass the time. Then we remembered back to our holiday, the previous year when we learnt how swim with our father Kenneth, when we were around our Aunt Nell's in Little Downham. Mum had left our father and was living with her new boyfriend Herbert; we wondered where we could go swimming in Ely.

We then remembered that there was an open air swimming pool, down by Ely railway station. The next day when we got up, we were sitting in the kitchen, and while we were having our breakfast our mother asked us what we were going to do that day. We told her we were going to go swimming, our mother then asked "And how are you going to afford that", Mothers boyfriend Herbert who was quietly eating his breakfast then spoke up "I will pay ". Herbert was a nice man and he wasn't short of a bob or two, as he owned his own farm. So as we were about to leave he handed Me, Diane and Owen a sixpence (2 and half P), each to go swimming. We all said thank you Herbert in chorus and gave him a kiss. We all trooped out the front door into Broad Street. The sun was shining brightly and it was really warm, as we made our way through the narrow streets of Ely, towards the old Railway station. We had swimsuits rolled up in our towels, tucked under our arms. After about half an hour, we reached Ely swimming pool, the swimming pool was surrounded by a big tall wooden fence and was entered by a single turnstile next to a wooden shed. We went up to the turnstile and paid our sixpences, to a big chubby friendly looking women, who sat on a big wooden chair. As we entered the swimming pool, the main pool seemed enormous to us as we had never seen it before. There were markers showing what was the deep end and markers showing you where the shallow end was.

There were also two diving boards, one low, and one higher and at the deep end there was a slide. After taking all of this in we headed towards the changing rooms. Diane and I headed towards the girls changing area and Owen headed towards the boys area, which was over by the deep end. The cubicles were like little wooden sheds, they had a couple of wooden benches to sit on, and a couple of clothes hooks to hang your clothes on, although you were not advised to leave any valuables in the cubicles. We changed into our swimming suits and headed towards the pool, after going though the footbath which was filled with disinfectant, we met up with Owen and headed past the baby paddling pool and towards the main pool. The main pool looked lovely and blue, I went down the steps first, into a shallow end followed by Owen and Diane. The water was quite cold even though it was a hot day but after a while we got used to it. We splashed around and then, we started to swim backwards and forwards across the shallow end. After a very long while we eventually had to go home, so we got out of the pool, and went back to the cubicles to get changed. On the way out we saw they had a big table by the turnstile, where they were selling orange squash, crisps and little bags of sweets. Such as black jacks and fruit salads, there was no way we could afford such luxuries, at least we could dream. We waited for Owen, and then we headed home for our tea, it was around this time that mum started to become friends with a women called Mary. She had taken Mary under her wing, when Mary's husband whose name was Albert all of a sudden committed suicide. It was thought that he had a severe mental breakdown. Albert was in business with a friend who worked as builders.

They did jobs in Broad Street and other various places in and around Ely. It was believed that Mum had meet Albert when he had done a job on our house, and they became more than friends. As well as leaving a wife Albert also left behind a daughter called Emma. Albert left his wife and daughter quite well off, with their own house and a little bit of money, Mary's daughter was very skinny and tall, she looked like a bean pole. Both of them were not quite all there, and they talked funny with stutters .People said Emma was like this because Albert and Mary had her quite late in life. Albert was in his early 50s and Mary was in her early 40s, and medical treatment wasn't very good in those days. Emma would always dress up in her miniskirts and platform boots on Thursdays and Saturdays when it was market days in Ely. She would then go up the market and try and sell favors to the farmers after they had been drinking. She then got into trouble with the police, when she tried to report one of the farmers who refused to pay. Her mother was so simple that she didn't realize her daughter was a prostitute.

After a couple more incidents she would eventually be taken into care, as she was only 13. Before this all happened Mary had asked our mum if Emma could hang out with Owen, Diane and me. We tried it for a while, but eventually we got fed up trying to keep her out of trouble, and also we had to share our sweets with her even though her mum wasn't hard up. After we had been going to the swimming pool a couple of times we started to get upset as we could never afford any of the sweets or drinks, which were laid out on the table, they looked so tempting to us. So the three of us had an idea of going through people's clothes that were hanging up in the cubicles, Owen would search the cubicles in the boy's area. Sometimes we would be lucky if we found a few odd pennies, here and there and we would be able to buy a couple of sweets and some days, we would get enough to buy a glass of orange squash as well. After this had been going on for a couple of weeks the people who had the money stolen reported this to the people who were in charge of the pool. The people in charge of the pool decided to do something about this; they planted a purse with a few pennies in the pocket of a dress and putting blue dye on the money. They left this dress hanging in the girl's cubicle and sure enough after a couple days me and Diane found the purse in the dress, we took the pennies and put them in our hands and to our horror our hands turned bright blue.

We then panicked and found the nearest drain to drop the pennies down; we then hurried to the toilets and tried to scrub the blue off our

Learn to Love Not Hate

hands. We scrubbed and scrubbed but it didn't matter how hard we tried the dye wouldn't come off our hands. We then done something really stupid, we went to the cubicle and got the dress and the purse and went and handed it in, to the chubby lady at the turnstile. She thanked us and then we hurried home thinking everything would be alright. Later that afternoon we sat down to eat our tea, and Diane and me were trying our hardest to keep our bright blue hands out of sight, when there was a loud knock at the door.

Mum got up and answered the door, after a few minutes of talking in the hall way, Mum entered with two enormous policemen. The older policeman who had three stripes on his arm, asked Diane and Me to put hands on the table right away. "A'HA" said the policeman caught blue handed, he then gave us a very long and severe telling off and told mum if she sorted it out it wouldn't go any further. Mum promised the police men she would sort it out. The two policemen strode out of the house leaving a very angry mum, and three terrified children. We got the hiding mum had promised the policeman and we were sent to bed not being allowed to finish our tea. We were also banned from the swimming pool for the rest of the holidays; if we didn't hand in the dress and purse we would have not been caught, as they wouldn't be able to trace us. When we got up the next morning, we were very sore and we didn't have any swimming to look forward too, so we had to find some other way to keep ourselves amused. The three of us decided to go down to the river, as you could always find something to do down there. We wandered up and down the river bank, we finally stumbled upon a nice little spot near the old bridge by the allotments.

The water was nice and clear and looked very inviting. As it was a really nice hot day, we decided to go for a swim. So we stripped down to our underwear and wandered into the cold water, then we started swimming and splashing about. It was very nice and quiet there with just the three of us and it didn't cost us a penny. After we had enough of swimming, we got out of the water and sat on the bank and dried out on the grass. After we discovered our little spot, we went down there a lot. We used to take our swimming costumes and towels and done it properly. All we needed now was some sweets; lady luck helped us out there. One morning we were walking past the allotments and someone was cleaning their hut out, we saw them throw tins onto the rubbish heap. When we got to the rubbish we picked the tins up and gave them a shake, you couldn't believe how disappointed we were, when we found out they were empty.

We were about to throw back into the rubbish when I noticed there was a red cross on the side of them, and a slot on the top. They were tins people used to collect money in, so we thought we would do some collecting of our own. We all grabbed a tin each and took it home, the next day after our daily swim we headed home for our dinner, after we had finished our meal, we got our tins out of their hiding places and decided to take our chances, and go collecting for the 'Red cross'(our sweet money). This went fine on the first couple of afternoons, we knocked on peoples doors and they would quite happily give us a couple of pennies in the tin. On the third afternoon we knocked on someone's door it was answered by big fat grumpy women. She looked mean and she spat as she talked, she opened her purse and grudgingly put in a penny in the tin. She then said " where's my little badge? ," you were meant to give them a little white badge with the red cross sign on it with a pin on the back. The three of us looked at each other very scared, we then ran to the next street and put our tins in the nearest bin, the grumpy old women was the first person to ask for a badge in three days, it was a good job we were in a strange street where nobody knew us, otherwise we would been in more trouble with the police and another good hiding from mum. The Red Cross would now have to do without us.

CHAPTER 20
.WILBURTON SCHOOL AND MY FRIEND CAROL.

When I was 10 years old I went to a normal secondary school, as we got no attention from are mother. Me, Diane and Owen had behavior problems, so we got sent to the manor school in Wilburton for children with special needs, in Ely Cambridgeshire. The headmaster was a, Mr Anderson, the children there really were backwards, there was lots of children with Down's syndrome, I used to look after one girl her name was Pat. I used to take her to the toilet and help her get dressed after physical education. She was 10 years old with dark hair and she had a really large head, she was a tubby well built girl. I used to take her to the toilets when she started her periods and made sure she put her pad on properly, she looked up to me and followed me about. I was acting like a mother even though I was at school. Pats mother was grateful for this; we used to go to Wilburton School on an old bus. We used to get on the bus at Gray's garage on the outskirts of Ely. I remember one day my brother Owen was teasing me, so I picked up a brick and was about to throw it, when a policeman grabbed the brick from behind me and gave me a right good telling off as this was 1960 and policemen done that then. Lots of children used to use the school bus, and we would have to go through all the little villages, to pick the children up. There was one strange boy called Brian and he used to stand in the middle of the road pretending he was driving a car. The lady who was supervising the bus had to get off the bus and put him on. I used to get in a lot of trouble on the bus, fighting with all the other kids and I was sent to the front of the bus to sit next to the bus driver, this was not unusual for me. There used to be about 35 children on the bus, it used to be packed.

They were really backward and they made a lot of noise, me being normal and just naughty made the most of it, and took advantage of it. I used to like going to Wilburton School because we used to go on nice trips. We used to have really lovely Christmas times there. On one particular trip which stands out in my mind is that we went to London, and we saw the old tea 'Clipper Cutty Sark' in Greenwich, we then went to the Tower of London and finished off with a cruise on the Thames, then we had tea and cakes, two teachers called Mr. Edwards and Mr. Davies took us on the trip. I remember one day at school Mr. Davis gave us some math's to do, I didn't do it and Mr. Davis was not very pleased, he said the only reason I was at Wilburton was because I was lazy and bone idle. I think the only reason why we played up so much at school was because we never got any attention at home. When it was sports day at the school, it was a really grand affair and they would put out a lovely selection of cakes out and also plenty of drinks, and we had a really nice time. Mum never came and watched any of us at sports day, even though all three of us were all pretty good at sports. The school dinners we had at the school were really nice and we really looked forward to the school dinners, we never had nothing that much when we were at home. Sometimes she would send me to bed with nothing at all to eat, she never treat Diane or Owen like this it made me feel really neglected. This was why I was really thin. When we used to wake up for school in the morning our stepfather would make us a breakfast of bread soaked in hot milk, served in a dish like a cereal. I used to detest this so I never ate it; by the time school dinner was served up I was really hungry.

The school dinner would usually last me till the next day especially if Mum sent me to bed without any dinner; it was as if she couldn't stand the sight of me. I had a friend at school called Carol, she was a funny girl, and she was very thin and very fragile. This was probably because she was a result of her Mother having sex with her own Brother. Her mother went to prison because of it, when she came out she had sex with her Brother again and now Carol had a brother. Carol lived on the same council estate as me; little did I know the sad ending she was going to have. In later years when I was 21 and married with 2 children of my own, I met up with Carol again. Carol had now married; she had got married because she was pregnant. Her husband was in trouble with the police because he had got caught stealing. They were living in a small bed sit. I told her to come round and see me, as we could become friends again.

I had a little boy called Terry who had just turned 1 years old; Carol wanted to know what it felt like to push a baby in a pram. So I used to let her push Terry in his pram round to her Mums and Dads, she used to really enjoy spending time with Terry, When Carol used to go to the hospital for an internal examination they used to have to knock her out as she was so scared. She was getting really close to having the baby and she used to come round mine and I used to wash and curl her hair. The next day she was going to the \R.A.F hospital in Ely to find out when the baby was going to be born. I went to visit her as she had to stay in and the baby was going to be started off, the next day I was in the kitchen and I heard a loud knock at the door.

I opened the door and a Woman from the health visitors was standing there, she told me that Carol had died during the birth of her baby, and the baby had passed away as well. This upset me and really broke my heart, I am glad I let her push Terry about in his pram as this was the only baby she got push in a pram. While this had happened her husband was in court, when they told him what had happened that Carol and the baby passed away, it upset him a lot and they had to send him to Forborne Mental Hospital in Cambridgeshire, were he suffered from a breakdown. My ex husband and I went to collect him and looked after him round ours, as Carols family didn't want anything to do with him. We looked after him and helped him arrange the funeral; we tried to comfort him so he didn't feel alone. Carol sadly had to be buried on unconsecrated ground as she was not christened. They were strict about things like that in those days. I was very upset, the next day I suffered from a breakdown, I had to get over it quick as I had two kids to look after. I miss her to this very day and will always love and remember her.

CHAPTER 21
.WORKING AT MRS. LAMPS.

It was 1963, Our Mother had been working as a house maid, in a big posh house in the posh part of Ely, is was up by the Cathedral. The house was nearly as big as the whole of Broad Street, were we lived. Mother had been working for professor and Mrs. Lamp for almost two years, unknown to me, as I showed as much interest in what she was doing as she did in what I was up to. As November approached and the nights started pulling in my sister would come home from school and after tea would walk into Ely to meet mum from work. While Diane was meeting Mum she got to meet Mrs. Lamp and Mr. Lamp they would give Diane and Mum old clothes which belonged to her and her daughter. After a while I noticed Diane was getting new clothes to wear, I then asked Mum where she was getting her clothes from and she told me. Funny that because I always wondered where she went after tea, I thought that sounded alright. So I started to join Diane on her walks and eventually I got to meet Mrs. and Mr. Lamp, because I was a bit older then Diane, Mrs. lamp asked me if I would like to earn a bit of pocket money, by helping Mum with a bit of cooking and cleaning, she said I could do this after school and on the weekends. The Lamps were very well of, and Professor Lamp would hold services at the Cathedral on the weekends and teach at Cambridge university during the week.

Mrs. Lamp did not need to have a job, so she use to fill her days up by doing charity work for charities such as the Red Cross. Mrs. Lamp would keep herself busy by organizing dinner parties and also holding cheese and wine parties, this made a lot of work for me and mother.

Mrs. Lamp would pay me really well and some weeks I would earn nearly 4 pounds, which used to be really good considering when I left school and started working at Woolworths I was only earning 4 pounds and 10 shillings for a whole week. Mr. and Mrs. Lamp were extremely rich and used to own several flats in Oxford; they used to rent them out to the students at the university. Professor and Mrs. Lamp had two children of their own, who were both grown up, the oldest one was 24 and he was a Royal navy officer, his name was Nicholas, we only got to see him when he came home on leave. His younger sister was Celia and she was away at Oxford university studying. We saw quite a bit more of her as they had a lot of holidays and she would always come home.

Celia had a horse which she rode a lot when she was home, and when she went back to university, she used to keep it in the stable down the road near the Kings School. Mrs. Lamp would go down and clean it out and feed it. I remember I was in the room going over some dusting and Mrs. Lamp came hobbling in, she was walking with a walking stick and her foot was all bandaged up. She told Mum how the horse got excited and jumped on her foot, I can't remember what the horses name was, but I'm sure it was not one of the ones Mrs. Lamp called it. When Mrs. Lamp used to hold one of her dinner parties there used to be a lot of guests and it would a be lot of extra work for me and Mum. Mrs. Lamp would always insist I do all the waiting on the Tables, she went out and brought me a nice smart black dress which she made me wear with a spotless white lace apron. After the guests had finished each course I would have to bring the plates, dishes and cutlery back to the scullery, where all the washing up was done.

The scullery was a big room which was very dark, as it was only lit by a little window and a very small light bulb. Down one side of the scullery was a big wooden table and down the other side was two big stone sinks, each of the sinks had a big wooden draining board. Down the far end of the scullery, high on the wall, there was a board, on the board there was a dozen shiny bells. Each of the bells was connected to little handles which connected to all the rooms in the house. These bells rung when they needed our services in that particular room. When I would be waiting on the tables, Mum would be washing the plates and

Diane would be drying them and stacking them on the table ready to be put up. When it was quiet Diane would go and sit on the little wooden chair in the corner, one day we were all in the scullery, Diane was sitting in the chair dozing off and suddenly three or four of the bells went off, Diane jumped and shouted out to Mum " THE ICE CREAM MAN , THE ICE CREAM MAN." Mum then said sit down you silly little girl. Mum then had to explain to Diane about the bells on the wall and what they did. Diane went red in the face and sat back on the chair, she was quiet for the rest of the night.

About six months after I had been working at Mrs. Lamps they had a new kitchen built and I never had to use the scullery again. Mrs. Lamp proudly showed me and Mum around the new furnished kitchen. The new kitchen was very big and the walls were painted cream white, a lot of light came through the big windows. Through the windows you could see a beautiful garden with flowers and an old plum tree, around the walls were polished units with polished marble tops. In the units was a built in oven and unknown to me a built in dishwasher. In the middle of the kitchen was a free standing hob, and under the windows was a pair of shiny stainless steel sink bowls.

One day I was standing in the new kitchen doing some washing up when all of a sudden there was a loud whooshing noise it made me jump out of my skin, I dropped the plate and it smashed into a thousand pieces. I went running out of the kitchen screaming" Mum, Mum ", and went straight into Mrs. lamp, she asked what the matter was, I told her and she laughed her head off. She then led me back into the kitchen and explained to me what the noise was. She explained to me about the dishwasher and how that it was rinsing the plates. By this time Mum had heard all the noises and she came into the kitchen, after we had cleaned up the plate we all had a cup of tea and a good laugh about it.

One Saturday when I was working at Mrs. Lamps, a very important man was coming to visit, his name was Bishop Walsh, he was coming to visit Mr. Lamp as it was approaching Christmas and they have a lot of important people preach at the cathedral at this time of the year. I was in the kitchen busy doing some jobs, and Mrs. Lamp came and approached me. She asked me to go and light the fire in the red room. The red room was called this because the walls the carpet, and all the

Learn to Love Not Hate

furniture were all different shades of red. Mrs. Lamp also had a blue room, a gold room and a pink room. Bishop Walsh was meant to arrive at the train station from London around dinner time, so Mrs. Lamp asked me to light the fire around 10'o'clock so it give it time to heat the room up. 10'o'clock soon came around and I made my way upstairs to light the fire, I was carrying a little basket of kindling, a box of matches and a newspaper rolled up under my arm. I got to the red room and set about starting the fire, I rolled up the newspaper and put it on the grate, then I laid the kindling neatly on top and the newspaper, after a while the kindling was burning nicely. So I laid some small logs on top. I left this burning nicely and went down stairs, to the backyard to fetch a basket of logs from the old woodshed.

When I got the logs, I went back upstairs and the fire was burning nicely, so I put some more logs on the fire and put a guard around the fire and left it. I went back downstairs carry on with my jobs. When I got downstairs Bishop Walsh had arrived and was sitting in the lounge with Mr. Lamp drinking a glass of sherry chatting away. Bishop Walsh was a grand looking old man who talked very posh. I quietly slipped into the kitchen and carried on with my jobs, preparing the dinner with my mum. After an hour or so Mrs. Lamp came bursting into the kitchen shouting "Valerie, Valerie," I thought I asked you to light the fire in the red room. I told her I had lit the fire, and left plenty of logs next to the fire so Bishop Walsh could feed the fire. Mrs. Lamp put her hand on her fore head and let out a gasp "No, No. Valerie people as important as Bishop Walsh do not feed the fire, you should have gone up and checked on the fire every hour or so. You had better go up and light the fire again please Valerie."

So after a lot of apologies I set off upstairs with my basket and a box of matches, leaving Mrs. Lamp to calm down by laughing it off with my Mum in the kitchen.

Whilst I was working for Prof. and Mrs. Lamp one of the jobs I got was to look after Prof. Lamp's mother who lived in the house with them, me and Mum used to jokingly say she used to live in the grey room. Mrs. Lamp senior was a very frail old lady with grey curly hair, she was very thin with long frail fingers although she was very grand looking, she must have been very pretty when she was younger. When I first got to meet her she was over a hundred years old, and to prove this she had her telegram from the Queen on the bedroom wall in a nice frame. Mrs. Lamp senior had a poodle called Trixie, which she kept in the room for company. Mrs. Lamp senior whose first name was Edith told me to call her Eady, and she kept her poodle in the traditional poodle hair cut, which I think made it look stupid. I didn't get on with the dog and it use to growl at me when I saw it, it must have heard me call it stupid. I used to have to take this poodle for regular walks and it used to play me up something rotten, because of this I used get the Mickey taken out of me by the King school boys as I had to walk past the college every morning as it was right near the house. In the morning I would take Eady her breakfast on a tray, She would have a bowl of corn flakes, and a pot of tea, when I would go back after a short while Eady had drunk her tea, but there was cornflakes all over the floor , she had put them on the floor for Trixie, but she did not eat them. I reckon that damn poodle didn't eat them so it would give me a job of cleaning them all up. Because Eady was so old Mrs. Lamp gave her suppositories and then Mrs. Lamp would tell me, to make sure she went to the commode every couple of hours. The commode was situated behind a big screen the other side of Eadys bedroom. To help me with this job Mrs. Lamp gave me an old brass alarm clock, which had to be wound up. Eadys bedroom was very large but did not have much furniture, just a bed, chest of draws, a chair and a wardrobe. In one corner there was small T.V. stood on a little table.

After Mrs. Lamp had given Eady her suppositories, and put her to bed. I would show Eady the times she would have to use the commode on my Brass clock. I would then go downstairs and continue on with my jobs leaving her settled in her chair or in bed watching the T.V. I would check on her very regularly, this turned out to be a bit of a game as Eady was too old to tell the time, I was not much better at telling the time as well. I left the clock on the chest of draws so we could both see it, sometimes I would go and check on her and she would be flat on the floor, where she had tried to stand up and use the commode, and other times she would be sitting on the chair with her knickers round her ankles as she thought she was on the commode. I would have to have a laugh at this. But the biggest disaster was yet to come, as someone forgot to wind up the brass clock and it stopped. I went and checked on her when I thought the two hours were up, but it was more like

Learn to Love Not Hate

three. As I entered the room there was a terrible smell, I guessed what it was straight away, there was Eady lying on her bed covered in it, her hands and her sheets were a mess. I thought I better move quick so I got bowl of water and got her night dress off, and washed her the best I could. I then put a clean night dress on her and changed the sheets, and hoped Mrs. Lamp would not notice.

On the weekends Prof. Lamp and Mrs. Lamp would travel away to Oxford, they would ask me to stay in the house over the whole weekend as Eady was in no fit state to travel. Mrs. Lamp would set up a camp bed in Eadys bedroom so I could hear if she wanted anything during the night, Mrs. Lamp was confident everything would be ok as the problem with the suppositories had been sorted out. Eady would always start to play up when she found out the Lamps were going away, she would tell Mrs. Lamp I couldn't stay with her as I was a 'Witch'. As I had long dark hair and very dark eyes. During the night after we had our dinner which Mum cooked I would say my goodbyes to Mum and Diane, I would then lock the doors and go up to Eadys room and settle down to watch the T.V. I remember one night as we settled down to watch the

T.V. we were watching Eadys favorite programme, it was an old black and white version of Sherlock Holmes, I remember at the time it was raining very heavily. We could hear the rain drops hit the skylight in the big room above Eadys room were Mrs. Lamp used to hold her tea dances, with the sound of the rain and the lightning flashing in the window, and also Trixie running about barking, it was almost like our own 'Hound of Baskervilles'. At the end of the night I was really scared and Trixie had to do without her walk, I would shut her in the kitchen for an hour and I would have to clean up after her, it was a lot easier and a lot less scary. With 'Sherlock Holmes', 'Trixie the poodle' and Eady going to the commode every two hours I was glad when the Lamps got back from Oxford, that meant I could go home and have a rest.

One Friday when I was at the Lamps she informed me she was expecting guests the next day, she told me to make sure the bed was made up in the pink room. She told me to make sure the room was well heated as the guest they were expecting was a missionary and he was from a really hot country, called Africa. She also told me his name was Mr. Omo, with all this information I went about making the beds and starting the fire, so it was roaring hot. The next morning a big posh car pulled up outside Mrs. Lamps front door, then Prof. Lamp, Mrs. Lamp, Mum and Me all lined up outside the house to greet him. As we were waiting Mrs. Lamp asked me did I wash Mr. Omos sheets, I must have misheard her " I washed the sheets in Daz, not in Omo because that's all we had ", I thought she said wash the sheets in Omo, Omo and Daz were both washing powders in the 1960s. Mr. Omo was a very nice man, who told us all types of wondrous stories about Africa, he told us about the natives and all about these strange animals such as Elephants with their trunks and giraffes with their long necks. We had never heard about these strange animals before, he also told us about his missionary work teaching the natives about God., because Mr. Omo was so friendly to us we made a special effort, looking after him for the week and made him feel very comfortable. When he left the following Saturday, he handed me a small brown envelope. I put this in my apron pocket, when he left I went into the kitchen. I made sure no one was there and I took the small envelope out my apron pocket and opened it, to my surprise, inside was 4 x 1 pound notes and a short message which read:-

"Thanks for Everything, Valerie"
Mr Omo

    I will never forget that as it was an extra whole week's wages as a tip, also he was one of the nicest men I had met at that time.
    One week that year Mrs. Lamp and the professor had to go to Oxford on business, so Mrs. Lamp suggested that I take a week off school and move into the house, as Prof. Lamps mother Eady still had to be looked after. As I was still only 13 years old, Mrs. Lamp suggested that my mother move in with me, even though I had taken most on the duties as my mother was heavily pregnant and couldn't manage to do a full day's work. So on Saturday morning when the Lamps were due to leave, mother and I stood on the front door step saying our goodbyes, Mrs. lamp handed me the keys to the house and a list of instructions,

Learn to Love Not Hate

there were such instructions, on how to turn the electric and water off, and to make sure all the windows and doors were locked at night times. Then they got in their big car and set off down the road. No longer they had left I heard the back door slam, I went running into the kitchen and standing there to my surprise stood, my Mum's husband Herbert and my brothers Owen, Arthur ,Bert and my sister Diane and in my stepfathers hand was a very large suitcase. After a while I got over the shock and said "What on earth are you doing here", Mum said it was alright they have come here to help, and besides it will save having to walk up here every day. Herbert then said "Come on girl, put the kettle on". So I accepted it and put the kettle on, and made the tea. We all sat around the big table drinking tea, and eating a jam sponge we found in the pantry. All in all the week turned out alright, with Herbert making the fires for me, and carrying the logs upstairs for me and the boys were old enough to do little jobs around the house. In return they would live like Kings and have fried breakfasts and roast dinners at nights all on Mrs. Lamps account, at the butchers. At night time we would all go round the house and make sure all the windows and doors were locked, and settle down to watch Mrs. Lamps T.V. set, with a big mug of chocolate and a big cream sponge mum had made. This was real treat for everyone as we didn't have a T.V. set at home.

We would take it in turns to check on Eady and she enjoyed the change of faces and she really hit it off with Herbert, he would be up there for ages sometimes and you could hear them both laughing their heads off. Friday night soon came around and we all had to muck in and have a really good clean up, they all had to leave the house as we didn't know what time the Lamps would return on Saturday. Good job they went as the Lamps arrived home early in the morning. Mrs. Lamp asked if everything went alright, I told her everything went fine, she went into the house followed by Prof. Lamp, she said "Well Done Valerie, Everywere looks Spotless". She then gave me a very large box of chocolates and said they were for looking after Eady and the house. After they had been home a few days Mrs. Lamp came up to me and said Eady had been talking about lots of people, keeping her company. I replied she must been having one of her funny turns, she also said she found a toy car on one of the chairs, teasingly she said " have you had one of your boyfriends round? ", Mum jumped into rescue me by saying she had it in her pocket and she must of left it behind by mistake.

One day when I was working I started to get a bit hot, Mrs. Lamp noticed this and she told me to go and get a glass of orange juice out the fridge in the kitchen, which was in the jug, already made up. When I got to the fridge there was two jugs in front of me. Mrs Lamp never mentioned this so I poured myself a glass with the first one I picked up and started drinking it, I noticed it had a funny taste but never thought nothing of it. About quarter of an hour later I started to feel dizzy and sick, and had to sit down. Mrs. Lamp asked what the matter was, I told her and she started laughing when she realized the mistake I had made. She explained she had made two jugs up, one of them was orange juice and the other one was Gin and orange. She had put them in the fridge so they would be nice and cold for the dinner party she was holding that evening. Mrs. Lamp then told me to sit down until I felt better; this was my first experience of alcahol. Mum heard all about this and decided to sample a couple of glasses herself, and to top the jug up with water. It didn't make her dizzy, mum liked a drink and sometimes would nip downstairs towards the big dining room they called the under craft, which had its own bar. She used to help herself to a couple of drinks she would always come back upstairs happier. When Mrs. Lamp had her new kitchen built it had everything except a washing machine, Mum and me thought this was odd. As it meant we had to waste a lot of time washing by hand, to do this we had to load all the laundry into baskets and take the baskets which were very heavy up three flights of stairs, to the bathroom. We then had to fill the bath full of washing powder and hot water and then scrub all the sheets, blankets, Prof. Lamps thick cotton long johns, by hand. When we done the shirts we had to really scrub the collars until they were spotlessly clean. We then had to empty the bath and rinse it out a couple of times, after we had done all that we had to put the laundry back into the baskets and take it down three flights of stairs into the back garden and hang it on the washing lines. All this used to take up nearly all the day and left us completely tired.

One day I was walking up the stairs with a bottle of bleach in my hand, I got half way up the stairs when I heard Mrs. Lamp shout out "Valerie the bottle is leaking", I looked behind me and there was

Learn to Love Not Hate

white spots on the dark blue carpet. I looked at the bleach bottle and sure enough there was a hole in the bottle, so I put my finger over the hole and ran downstairs towards the kitchen sink, leaving Mrs. Lamp shouting at me to get a bucket of water and a scrubbing brush. I returned quickly with a bucket and a brush, and set to work immediately washing the bleach off the carpet. I think I got most of it, but when it dried if you looked carefully you could see little white spots on the carpet. Mrs. Lamp calmed down after a while, then she said next time I take bleach upstairs I would have to put in a carrier bag. Another time I was walking through the hallway humming away and swinging my arms, when my hand went bashing into Prof. Lamps bowler hat and causing a dent, I looked around and luckily no one saw, so I ran upstairs and got Eadys dog 'Trixie' and put her on a lead, I then went to Prof. Lamps study and informed him, Trixie had knocked his hat off and treaded on it. I handed him the hat, he just laughed and punched his hat on the inside and it returned to its normal shape, if I had known that I would have done it myself and not blamed \Trixie. Another time in the kitchen Mrs. Lamp had bought a different kind of tea, it was called "China Tea ", and Mrs. Lamp informed me she would be drinking this in the future, so later that day when it was time to make the afternoon tea, I put the tea leaves in the teapot and poured the hot water in as normal, and I let it stand for five minuets, I then went to pour it out and it still looked pale yellow. So I gave it a good stir and I let it stand for another five minutes, I then went to pour it out and it was still pale yellow, I thought the tea was faulty so I poured the pot of tea away, then I made another pot of tea. This time I added a couple extra spoons of tea leaves, After five minutes the result was the same. I then got fed up with this and went to find Mrs Lamb and told her I couldn't get the tea to brew properly, she just sat there laughing and told me that sort of tea didn't go brown. I wish she had told me that before then I wouldn't had felt stupid. It was around this time I started to get letters from the King school boys asking me out and telling me they fancied me, I felt really embarrassed by those letters and after a while I told Mrs. Lamp about the letters.

She explained she had trouble with these before and they had probably mistaken me for her daughter Celia, after Mrs. Lamp had a word with the head master of the King school the letters stopped coming, in a way I was slightly disappointed. Another job we got roped into doing was cooking Bishops Walsh's meals, when he was at home. Mrs. Lamp asked us to do this because he was away quiet a lot of the time and it wasn't worth him employing a cook, he had a big house almost next door, I thought this was a bit of a cheek, but Mum didn't mind as she used this as a excuse to cook Herbert and the kids a meal as well, and put it Bishops Walsh's account. God she was crafty.

In the New Year Mrs. Lamp had the builders in again, this time they were converting the room above the kitchen into a flat, they installed a bathroom with running hot water and placed a little kitchen in there, and also a new bed. It was quiet a nice cosy little flat. I asked Mrs. Lamp who the flat was for and she said it was for me for when I left school, I could live there rent free and she would find me a nice rich farmer's son to settle down with. It all sounded very nice but as time moved on the idea sounded more and more terrible. I would be working all the hours god sent and because I would be living there I would be at Mrs. Lamp's beck and call. I would never have time to see my friends or that rich farmers son, so as school leaving time approached I said my thank you's and goodbyes and moved on to pastures new, but I will never forget the memories of working at Mrs. Lamps.

Chapter 22
.The Start, Middle and End of Mums and Dads Life .

During the summer of 1932, among growing unrest in Europe caused by an evil Dictator named Adolf Hitler, which eventually led to the Second World War, a little girl was born in Cambridgeshire. The little girl's name was June Rose May; She was born on the 23rd of June 1932. She was the loving daughter of Robert and Lucy Lyles. June was born into a loving family in Ely, and lead a perfectly happy childhood, going to school, and playing happily with her friends. Although times were hard, June and her two brothers were all fed and looked after properly. All went well in life and she done alright at school, she left school in 1947 when she reached the age of 15. After her school life was over, she found herself a job on the local farm, doing a bit of housekeeping. The farmer was probably one of her dad friends and he got her the job. June had been working at the farm for about a year and a half, when she become friendly with one of the young farm laborers, his name was Kenneth Winters. After going out on a few dates, they fell in love and started going steady. One day in late August, June was surprised to discover she was pregnant. She told her boyfriend Kenneth the news, Kenneth took the news better then June expected. He wasn't a bit upset and he decided him and June better do the right thing, the next day after work they walked to Ely, to see Junes Mum and Dad.

When Kenneth told June's Dad the news, he asked for her hand in marriage. June's dad went berserk and started punching Kenneth in the face. Junes Mum stepped in and broke them apart; Kenneth was covered in blood, and had a lovely Black eye. Junes parents didn't believe in abortions, and they told June to have the baby and they would help her cope and also, help her raise the baby . June and Kenneth didn't stand for any of that, and they decided they were going to get married. After things calmed down, June's parents realized they could not stop them. So they decided to help them, so just after Christmas in 1950. June's Dad moved Kenneth and June into a small cottage in Silver Street, in Ely. It was agreed that Kenneth paid Junes Dad some rent each week. A month before the baby was due June and Kenneth got married, they tied the knot in Ely Register Office. It was small ceremony with just each set of parents there, with a couple of Kenneth's friends there acting as witnesses. I don't think June had many friends, as she was stuck working on a remote farm, and she spent all of her free time with Kenneth.

Things went smooth at Silver Street leading up to the birth, and on the 20th May aged 17 years and 11 months June gave birth to a beautiful little girl, which she named 'Valerie Ann'. When June came out of the Grange Hospital in Ely, with her new baby Valerie in her arms, she returned back to the cottage in Silver Street and carried on with her new family life, with Kenneth Winters and Baby Valerie Ann. Sadly things started going downhill, and the all the abuse and despair started. Kenneth started Hitting Mum, and shouting at her for the tiniest little things. He just generally treat her really bad. June was still sore from the child birth, and when Kenneth couldn't have sex when he wanted it, he would viciously rape her on the kitchen floor, whilst new born baby Valerie slept peacefully in her cot. It was after one of these horrific rapes that June found out she had fell pregnant again, she found out she was pregnant in July 1950 just 3 months after little Valerie was born. Mother went through Hell when she was carrying the baby and in April 1951 she gave birth to bouncing baby boy she named ' Owen '.

Just before little Owen was born Kenneth had stated to play up, and he had not paid Junes Father the Rent they agreed on. Junes father

Learn to Love Not Hate

had been hearing a lot of stories on how Kenneth had been treating his daughter June, So Junes Dad Quite bluntly confronted Kenneth and told him to get the Hell out of Silver Street. June would move back in with her parents with the babies; this was not to be as Kenneth had landed himself a job. This job was in a nearby town of March, the job was as a farm hand and a tied cottage came with it. The next day Kenneth's Dad turned up in his little black car, and drove Kenneth, June and the two babies to March, so they could settle in their new cottage. June settled into her new life and things went alright for a little while, but things were about to turn really bad for her. One evening she was busy in the kitchen, when there was a loud knock at the door. June answered the door, stood in front of her was two policemen. One of the policemen informed her that Kenneth had been arrested on an alleged rape, of a young local girl. June was told that Kenneth had grabbed the girl, who was walking and pulled her into a field, he had then tied her to a tree and then forced himself on her. Kenneth was being held at March police station and would face the local magistrates in the morning.

That day June turned up at the court to hear that Kenneth was being remanded in custody accused of rape. During the next couple of months leading up to his trial at Cambridge Crown Court, June went and saw him a couple of times, leaving the children with her Mum and Dad. When the case came up in court, Kenneth was found guilty and sentenced to 2 years in jail. Kenneth was carted off to prison, but before he went he learned that June had fell pregnant again. June went back to the cottage in March, where the kind farm owner let her live until things got sorted out. There was no social security in those days, but she lived there quite comfortable with help from her Mum and Dad, and also Kenneth's Parents. Kenneth's Dad drove June to Prison a couple of times to see Kenneth. June visited Kenneth until January 1952, when she had to stop as she was heavily pregnant with her latest addition, as she found it too uncomfortable to travel. In June 1952, she was taken to the Grange Hospital where she had her previous babies. After a couple of days she gave birth to a little girl she named 'Diane '. June was released from the Hospital and she returned back to the

Cottage, Valerie and Owen then returned home from their Granny's to their Mum and new born Diane. June seemed happy to be a Mum.

After a couple of months she seemed to be strong enough to travel, so she went to prison to see Kenneth. She showed Kenneth a picture of their new baby girl Diane. Kenneth was over the moon and nearly in tears. The months passed by and Christmas came, June went and saw Kenneth a couple more times, on one of the Visits June had some bad news for him, The farm owner told June that he needed the tied cottage back for one of his workers and he wanted her to move out in a month. So June got in touch with the council and told them she would be homeless in a month, the council acted quite quickly. Three weeks later they fixed her up with an asbestos prefab in the village of Witchford. Witchford was about five miles outside of Ely, When she went to see Kenneth she told him about the new house and how it was located in a different Village. She told him they could start of fresh, when he was released from prison. Kenneth seemed pleased about this. When Kenneth was released from prison in January 1953, he went to his new home in Witchford. He was very impressed with it and how June had set herself up, and how she had cared for three children.

What Kenneth wasn't impressed with was all the weight June had put on. June then to admit it wasn't fat she had put on; in fact she was carrying another child. She had to tell Kenneth she had fallen to temptation and she had an affair. She wouldn't tell Kenneth who her lover was, but it was all over with. When Kenneth heard this he went absolutely crazy and gave her the biggest beating of her live, leaving her black and blue and very sore, luckily she didn't break anything or lose the baby. June had gone to hospital as June was very hurt, and the doctor feared for the baby. June must have loved Kenneth because she wouldn't say how she got the injuries; if she had Kenneth would have gone back to prison. Kenneth calmed himself down a lot after that and he got himself a job, on one of the farms in Witchford. June soon recovered and she continued with her family life. In March 1954 she was admitted to Bowthorpe maternity Hospital, where she gave birth to a baby boy. She named him 'Elwin'. Kenneth was not very pleased but he took the baby on as one of his own. Elwin was a happy little boy but the Doctors said he wasn't quite normal, June thought this was to do with the beatings she received from Kenneth, but she kept this to herself. At the end of November 1954, disaster hit the prefab in Whitchford as baby Elwin came down with T.B. Meningitis, he was admitted to hospital where he passed away on the 7th December 1954 aged just 20 months.

Even more bad news was yet to follow, the health authority informed June and Kenneth that all the clothes and bedding would have to be burnt and their little house would have to be demolished. June and Kenneth took this in their stride and they all moved to another cottage on the outskirts, as Kenneth found himself another job. June seemed to fit into her life pretty smoothly, until February 1955 when June found herself pregnant again. June took things a little bit steadier this after what happened to baby Elwin in November 1954. She gave birth to another boy she named Robert, she then returned back to her new home. Kenneth didn't seem so pleased this time. Kenneth had returned to his old ways and the beatings, rapes and abuse carried on. It got to November 1956 and June decided things couldn't go on the same way, after the New Year. She rung up Kenneth's Mum and Dad who lived at the bank in Little Downham, and told them she is leaving Kenneth for good. June was so upset and heartbroken when she was on the phone to them, that they jumped in the car and visited June straight away. As soon as they arrived June picked up baby Robert and ran out the house explaining she couldn't take another beating of Kenneth, he would kill me this time she explained. June got a neighbor to take her back to her parents house in Broad street. June never said goodbye to her other three kids, Valerie, Owen and Diane. They eventually ended up in a children's home in East Dereham. June tried to visit them as much as possible.

Valerie, Owen and Diane were there for three years, when it was time to come out of the children's home, Robert and Lucy Lyles tried their best to sort their daughter June out. They had moved out of No70 Broad Street and they took Robert with them. They gave the No70 house to June to bring her children up in, so they could live like a proper family. Meanwhile June never had much to do with Kenneth, and they got divorced. Kenneth's life didn't get much better and he ended up in prison twice more, once in 1961 he got a sentence of two months for assault on a person in a pub after he had been drinking again, and again in 1963 he ended up in Wormwood scrubs after appearing at the Old Bailey in London, Convicted for rape again. Valerie only saw Kenneth once more, that was in the summer of 1966, Kenneth walked into Woolworths in Ely after he found out where she worked, and got her a trouser suit as a late Birthday present, I don't know if Kenneth saw June in Ely but someone must of told him Valerie worked there. After that Kenneth moved to Kings Lynn where he remarried, and had some more children.

His abusing and beating continued with his new family. Kenneth eventually died a slow and painful death, of Prostrate Cancer in 2007 at the age of 76; God paid him back in the end. Meanwhile June was living a half decent life at No70 Broad Street. She met and married a local farmer, his name was Herbert Johnson. She was married to Herbert for 21 mostly happy years. She had another 3 children their names were, Bert, Arthur and Herbert Jnr. Despite their happy marriage June had her little affairs and didn't treat her children very well especially Valerie, but Herbert was a good man and he tried to make up for her cruelty. In 1982 tragedy struck June again, and Herbert died of a brain Hemorrhage. He was 76, this particularly upset oldest daughter Valerie as she loved him a lot. She loved him more than her real father, and it took her along time to get over the death. The death upset June as well but not as much as Valerie, as June remarried to a local man, his name was Michael Garner.

June settled down quite a lot with her new husband Michael, this was probably because all of her kids were grown up by now, and had left home. They had been married for 4 years until one day Michael came home from work, and June had passed away whilst she was in the garden. June had died in the Garden of a Heart attack whilst she was hanging the washing out. June died on the 6th October 1987 she was 55 years old. June died a few hundred yards away from her final resting place in Ely cemetery. June had found peace at last. June was not a bad women or a mother, it was just that life dealt her a bad hand in the form of an evil man. Most of June's children were from a result of rape not love, and when you given something you don't want, you tend to resent it instead of looking after it. Everything happened too soon and she was too young to deal with a strong and violent man, who would stop at nothing to satisfy himself. But he paid the price in the end. At least June had a few happy years with Herbert and Michael, and she didn't have to suffer much in the end. One child of hers, she treated the worst is now the only one who visits her grave regularly with flowers, with her husband and children is her oldest daughter Valerie. She learnt to love not hate.

Printed in the United Kingdom by
Lightning Source UK Ltd., Milton Keynes
140722UK00001B/46/P